The Power of Prayer A Personal Conversation with God

By

Lorenzo C. Spencer

I0233649

The Power of Prayer A Personal Conversation with God

© Copyright 2012, 2013 All rights reserved worldwide by
Lorenzo C Spencer

Spencer Truth Publishing

ISBN-13: 978-0615828015

Second Edition Paperback

Scripture quotations marked (NKJV) are taken from the New
King James Version®. Copyright © 1982 by Thomas Nelson, Inc.
Used by permission. All rights reserved.

Scripture quotations marked (NIV) are taken from the Holy
Bible, New International Version®, NIV® Copyright © 1973,
1978, 1984, 2011 by Biblica, Inc. Used by permission. All rights
reserved worldwide.

Scripture quotations marked (NIV1984) are taken from the Holy
Bible, New International Version®, NIV® Copyright © 1973,
1978, 1984 by Biblica, Inc. Used by permission. All rights
reserved worldwide.

All rights reserved. No part of this publication may be
reproduced, stored in a retrieval system, transmitted in any form
or by means-electronic, mechanical photocopy, recording, or any
other- except for brief quotation in print reviews, without the
prior permission of the publisher and author.

The Power of Prayer A Personal Conversation with God is a non-fictional book on prayer, but I
used fictional characters and situations in my parables to convey a message.

When I use the phrases or words, "*at work, before work, my job, my supervisor, my new supervisor, or upper management,*" it isn't
referring to a certain time span or people within a certain time span, but it may cover several instances within my entire
work history. There are no specifics on which job, what supervisor and upper management, or where those things took place
because that is irrelevant. Those above phrases or words are blank phrases meaning left up to the reader imagination.

Printed in the United States of America

Acknowledgements

I would like to thank our Heavenly Father for his son and for the opportunity of receiving salvation and truth. I would like to thank our Heavenly Father for allowing me the opportunity to write this message. I understand that I have no knowledge at all, but I know all by wisdom through Jesus Christ. I thank God for letting his Holy Spirit guide me in all truth and using me to give his children a word. I thank God for allowing me to learn and experience different scenarios doing my writing, so I could understand better. I thank God for allowing me to stay true to his word so that people could relate to this book.

I would like to thank my editors RENITA COLEMAN, ANQUENETTE SPENCER, AND SHALETHA DAVIS because they did such a magnificent job. I sincerely appreciate their hard work to the cause.

I would like to thank my wife and daughter. My daughter touched my heart because when I was writing she said, "Daddy, I'm going to write a book too." When I began to pick up my pen, she would grab her notebook with a pen and start writing as well. There is nothing like a father having a great relationship with his child. I would like to thank my family for supporting and putting up with me while allowing me to listen to God and follow my purpose. I would like to thank everyone who saw the vision and encouraged me to follow through till the end.

I would like to thank my mother who has given me so much inspiration to do good things. I thank her for taking such good care of me. As a child, I was a handful. I was blessed because I had the luxury of being a son to my brother's and sister's father who claimed me as their own. I claim them as my own too and give thanks to them for making me feel like a son. I would like to give thanks to my stepfather who I call my father. He has taught me so much and we have shared many things on my spiritual and natural journey.

I would like to thank my father and stepmother for being a part of my life. I give thanks to everyone who shared with me on my journey that had a part in my life. Some played a very small part and others impacted my life greatly. I would like to thank my brothers and sisters in Christ. I would like to thank my grandparents, uncles, aunties, cousins, nieces, nephews, grandnephews, mother-in-law, brother-in-laws, and sister-in-laws. I would like to thank God for the family he gave me. Our bond is very unique because of the experiences we shared. Oh yes, I would like to thank my sisters and brothers. Who I respect deeply, and I will always cherish their inner beauty.

I would like to give thanks to my original pastor and all the churches that have allowed me to sit in their congregation and learn some truth. I would like to thank anyone who sent up a prayer for me on this project that I might operate in integrity of the truth. It just won't be right without thanking my friend Jay who got me into thinking outside the box. We had plenty of enlightened conversations.

Psalm 66:19-20 (NIV)
19 but God has surely listened
and has heard my prayer.
20 Praise be to God,
who has not rejected my prayer
or withheld his love from me!

Psalm 116:1-2 (NKJV)
116 I love the Lord, because He has heard
My voice and my supplications.
2 Because He has inclined His ear to me,
Therefore I will call upon Him as long as I live.

Contents

Prayer is an intimate fellowship with our Father (Jehovah God)

We Come

Father, we come to you in praise

Thanking you for you

Thanking you for the many blessings

You have spoken over our life

Father, we come to listen

To hear from our Father of love

Father, we come to intercede

We pray for our loved ones

We pray for our sisters and brothers

Who stand in need of a word from you today?

Father, we come asking to hear from you

Father, we come confessing our sins

Father, we come to ask for a righteous mindset

So, we can receive all of our blessings from you

In Jesus mighty name we come

Surrendering all to you

Chapter 1

Do We Know Our Father?

A lot of people go through life not knowing the Father. They know about the Father. However, never take time to build a personal relationship with him. They are as distant as a child who met his father once in his lifetime. He knows of his father but never truly discovers anything about his father.

They are so disconnected spiritually and emotionally because of the limited involvement with the Father. They never take time to study his word. They never take time to seek him in prayer. Some of his children feel like they don't need their Father. They figure that they can make it through life on their own.

They are self-made. Everything revolves around them. They won't even acknowledge that there is a God. Let alone that he is their Heavenly Father. If they acknowledge him, it is only to receive a request from him while in the middle of life's turmoil.

There are others who know their Father in a natural sense. They get caught up in the stealthiest sin. They feel that their Father won't accept them back home because he warned them of the danger. Sin blocks their thoughts. They can't think straight. In the middle of the blockage, they don't know how to start or maintain a personal relationship with the Heavenly Father.

A personal relationship with our Heavenly Father may seem complicated. Almost impossible to the ones who don't know what a true relationship is. A lot of times, we don't understand the meaning of a relationship. We think, "A good relationship is entirely about receiving gifts." We think, "It's all about the other people pleasing us, listening to us, and giving in to our will."

We don't know how to build a good relationship with our mother or brothers. I can see why that it may seem difficult to start building a personal relationship with God. I know it might seem to be out of reach. It is more in reach then our next breath. For his children, obtaining a relationship has always been in our vicinity. Through reading his word and praying, we can begin to make a connection with our Heavenly Father.

God's word can take on a new meaning in our life. It can illuminate every dark spot in our life. God's word reveals to us truth. It is the truth. In order to put it in its proper context, we must be led by his Holy Spirit. If we are not guided by his Holy Spirit, then it is almost like reading a blank sheet of paper without the spiritual insight. Through prayer, we can understand his spiritual reality by asking him for understanding. When we read his word, it will increase our understanding of God because God's Holy Spirit will guide us.

Our prayers are like fertilizer. It cultivates our life like it gives grass and flowers the strength to grow. Our prayers give us the strength to keep pushing forward. When our matters get worse, our ego bruises, or our perfect life has an interruption in a split of a moment; our prayers will give us the determination to improve our crisis. Without fertilizer, plants and flowers still grow. They have the possibility to grow beautiful with strong roots and water. Without a strong prayer life, a person can still grow. A person has the possibility to still grow if he or she has strong spiritual roots. They can still grow if they drink fresh true water from the knowledge of the truth. Fertilizer maximizes the plants or flowers chances to grow to be magnificent. A strong prayer life maximizes our natural and spiritual life to be glorious.

Even the world knows that the best way to build a relationship is through communication. Prayer is communication with our Heavenly Father. Our Heavenly Father is Jehovah (Yahweh). Prayer is the building block of building a personal relationship with God. Through prayer, we are connected with the Heavenly Father. We can fulfill our loneliness through exchanging a few words with him. It is our way of expressing our thoughts, finding comfort, and appreciating his generosity toward us. It is a foolproof way of getting to know our Father by conversing, asking questions, and searching his will for our life.

2 Corinthians 1:3-4(NKJV)
3 Blessed be the God and Father of our Lord Jesus Christ, the Father of mercies and God of all comfort, 4 who comforts us in all our tribulation, that we may be able to comfort those who are in any trouble, with the comfort with which we ourselves are comforted by God.

We can contact our Heavenly Father at any time and about any circumstances. This is a blessing and reason to celebrate. We learn to tap into our benefits through prayer. My daughter always tells me, "Daddy I didn't know" to escape punishment. She will never know if our relationship stays uncultivated. She will never get to know what I expect of her if we are too busy to share information. I have to find time to fulfill her needs for conversation. She has to fit me in her schedule in order, for us to grow as a family. We have to make time for our daily conversation with the Lord. There is always a sacrifice to be made if we put our whole heart in something. God put his whole heart in it when he sacrificed his son for us on the cross.

John 3:16 (NKJV)
16 For God so loved the world that He gave His only begotten Son, that whoever believes in Him should not perish but have everlasting life.

We have no excuse as being children of God. He is never too busy to listen and respond to his children. There are some who don't want to put in the time to share with him. We set aside time for everything else that is meaningless. When it comes down to cultivate a relationship with God through prayer, it is a problem for some people. If he thought about us that way, some of us wouldn't exist. We should praise him just for the thoughts of us.

When we pray, we can understand his plan for our lives. We can understand our destiny. If we never inquire about our purpose, we may never understand our purpose.

Prayer enlightens our overview on different scenarios that we face in our lives. Prayer builds strength, patience, and character. It is the very essence of the Holy Spirit breathing into our life. It is a fresh breath of divine love flowing from the Father.

Prayer is a Christian's most valuable tool. It is our way of speaking to such a loving Father. Our Father will provide good things to all his children no matter if they deserve it or not. A lot of times, we don't deserve his goodness. God provides us with our basic needs anyway. God desires us to pray everywhere in love while trusting him. God longs for our prayer requests.

1 Timothy 2:8 (NKJV)
8 I desire therefore that the men pray everywhere, lifting up holy hands, without wrath and doubting;

God is able to do any and everything accordance to his will. Sometimes we pray for things contrary to the Father's will while hoping to receive it. The minute we line our prayers up along with what the Father wants us to do, then we will receive everything that is good for us. We must obey his commandments. While believing with faith, that he is able and will provide us with his good things. God specializes in the impossible. Our Heavenly Father is still in the miracle business. We unlock his wonder working power through prayer.

1 John 3:22(NKJV)
22 And whatever we ask we receive from Him, because we keep His commandments and do those things that are pleasing in His sight.

Mark 10:27(NKJV)
27 But Jesus looked at them and said, "With men it is impossible, but not with God; for with God all things are possible."

Lots of people pray but don't obey. They miss the mark because obeying gives us the positive results. We can expect to receive good things from our Father. When we don't obey his commandments, the direct line is broken. Communication gets through, but it is weak.

Just like a cell phone that roams to find a tower, the tower of our prayer signal is weak due to sin. We must stay connected to life's tower by repenting of our sins. Sometimes our batteries might die out when we disobey God. We must pray to recharge our thoughts with his presence.

Building up a Relationship

Let us look at relationships for a minute. No relationships are perfect. There is almost in all cases one who gives a little more, and one who gives lesser. Even in the mix of the difference, the relationship still last most of the time. If one is willing to push harder, then the other person finally gets it. A relationship takes hard work. Our natural relationship might not be perfect. We can find a perfect relationship in God through Jesus. We can reach our echelon through following his lead and guidance. He will pay attention to us and listen to us. God will always have time if we need a shoulder to cry on. He will never forsake us and surely will help us. Regardless of our countless disappointments, God will always love us. We just have to stay under God's covering. He will draw near to us in our silent cry wallows. Our Heavenly Father will keep our spiritual eye in the right perspective. We can share our awkwardness and loss of hope with him. In our daily conversation with him, God will restore us. The minute we draw away from sin.

Sometimes our family is unresponsive to our problems. They look up in praise when everything going well. The minute your life shift and your image are tarnished your family will disown you. It can be a traumatic experience to encounter alone. That is why it is important to have an established relationship with the Heavenly Father. Through our knowledge of him, we won't miss a beat. It won't dampen our spirit because we know how to repent and pray for the state of affairs to come to pass. The instant we have fostered not just any relationship but a loving relationship when we are down his words can encourage us. The Holy Spirit reshapes our depressed spirit and liberates our discomfort with joy and ecstasy.

Always been Present

God has always been present in our life. We may have been unconscious of how God has been working in our lives. We may have been too self-absorbed or dumbfounded to know better. We can't let other people stupor, or our pity parties separate us from God. Through prayer, we slowly discover the genuine nature of his presence. After the moment we intake his countless blessings, then it may open up our eyes to see the truth. If we are unwilling to communicate, then it may cause us to stay stuck in darkness. The moment we partake of God's glory our life changes for the best. We must hold fast to the initial embrace of God's touch over our life.

We must keep the connection to the source by talking to him as often as possible.

It is easy to destroy a relationship when all communication ceases. You don't know how to please one another. You don't know what bothers the other. It is a recipe for failure. A life without prayer is a recipe for failure too. When we cease to communicate with the Heavenly Father, we keep ourselves from the knowledge of his will.

Once we enter back in his presence, we become more spiritually aware of the deep meaning of it. Our consumption of his presence during our praying time invites his Holy Spirit to bless our lives. We begin to see past our environment because our spiritual eyes see past our conditions. God gives us the strength to take advantage of our environment and not let it take advantage of us. We gain his knowledge in our common sense by the Holy Spirit. While we are in fellowship with him daily, our knowledge increases, as well as our love. We feel no absence of his presence because in prayer God is present.

The Secret Place

The person who dwells in prayer is in the secret place of the almighty. He or she will abide in the presence of the almighty. Just knowing the man or woman of prayer dwell in the presence of God, should make us want to bathe in his presence. Prayer is the secret place because in prayer we correspond with the Father. While communicating with the Father, we learn about him and slowly build up a personal relationship with him. In building that relationship, we learn how to shed off sin.

We learn how to immerse in his love. We learn how not to fear, but how to adore and worship the Lord. The source of true power is God. He is love, so love is power. We can learn it through prayer. In his secret place, we abide under his shadow. His shadow is a refuge from danger or observation of our life.

Psalm 91:1(NKJV)
91 He who dwells in the secret place of the Most High Shall abide under the shadow of the Almighty.

Matthew 6:6(NKJV)
6 But you, when you pray, go into your room, and when you have shut your door, pray to your Father who is in the secret place; and your Father who sees in secret will reward you openly.

The Blessing of Prayer

It is a blessing within itself to be able to build a personal relationship with God. We may not have the president, prime minister, or the royal family on speed dial, but we have a direct connection to Our Heavenly Father through prayer. Our Heavenly Father is everything that we need. There is nothing more precious than talking with the one who completes us.

Do we ever consider how blessed we are? Some people are so busy with their everyday hustle and bustle that they don't realize God. In this day and time, we are charged for just about everything we do. There is a charge for water, air, to learn, and some places may charge you to walk down the street. In our society driven by monetary gain, it is a blessing to be able to call on God for free. We ought to shout Hallelujah. It doesn't cost us anything to communicate with the creator of the universe. We have no excuse, but some of us are trapped by blindness.

Unlocking Life Mysteries

The key to unlocking life mysteries is prayer. We can unfold a world that we never knew. We can learn to accept things that won't change. We can learn how to change things that are changeable. Our destiny lies in our prayers. Our future begins to look brighter because we understand on a spiritual level. Our parents don't hold the key to our life. Our Heavenly Father holds the key to our life, and he has provided us with two doors. Which one will you choose? We can learn to uplift God more while doing so downplaying self. Through Jesus we can reconnect with self because we are powerful through him.

We are spiritually dead if we don't allow the Holy Spirit an opportunity to breathe. Prayer is a necessity to create a new life in our old life. We must focus on spiritual peace and not immerse ourselves in seeking material things. There isn't anything wrong with asking for worldly joy if we do it with moderation. We must remember to seek God in prayer. We have to indulge our spiritual senses as well as our worldly senses.

When indulging our spiritual sense by using life's key, we can open the door. The door is the word of God. It is like any ordinary door. However, on the other side is life. Life eternity is for the children who understands and keeps his commandments. We all have access through Jesus. If we don't understand how our access badges work, we discover it through prayer and by reading the bible.

The bible is the most important book in our life if we choose to read it. It can be nonsense, for the one who don't search for God in prayer. A child could be wiser than any learned man if they seek God in prayer first because true wisdom comes from God's word not earthly books. Once you read the bible after praying, the mysteries begin to unfold. The spiritual side of the word is revealed along with the natural side of the word. The things that seem to make no sense now make perfect sense.

You are enlightened by the spiritual influx from the Holy Spirit. All truth will shine forward for you to grab hold of it. It has already been at your reach. The truth was locked in the pages of the scriptures for the spiritual man. The natural man will always have a hard time of understanding. Because his self-will dictates what is true or not leading him in a false representation of the truth.

In Jesus Name

The Spencer family shared a treasure vault with all sorts of valuables in them. The vast wealth was collected over the many years from different members of the family. Someone had 96 gold bars and another relative had 32 expensive diamond earrings. They had so much money on hand that it was impossible to count it all within 100 days. They all knew the password to unlock the family vault. Because it was part of the family bank but kept in a secret second vault. One day a grandson changed the passwords.

The vast wealth served no one any good because the grandson went hiking for a year on a secluded island. No one had anyway of contacting him. Their riches brought them great fame and authority. But without the passwords to the vault and the electronic account, they were powerless. They had no money to make the necessary trades to keep their riches intact. After the grandson returned, just about all their wealth was lost except of the tangible treasures. The paper money was used to cover their extensive amount of debt that had built up in the grandson's absence.

We as Christian have an infinite natural and spiritual wealth in Jesus. As soon as, we ask our Heavenly Father in prayer for things that lines up with his will. Jesus is our avenue to get those things. When we fell to use our password or somehow forget the password, we might come up short. Then our infinite natural and spiritual riches in the Lord serve us no purpose in our heart vault. Our password has authority over the seen and unseen principality that we war against each day. There is a considerable amount weighed on the proper password or in our instance the phrase, "In Jesus Name." Here is the catch clause 22. You can't use the same password for another person's account. It must be the correct account to be able to receive the contents in the vaults. After every prayer, we should finish with the phrase, "In Jesus' name." We must use it in according with the Father's will in order to receive the contents of our prayers answered. This is our approved account by the Father. Our heart must have the substance rooted in love, or we will spiritual bankrupt ourselves. Then the phrase, 'In Jesus' Name" has no effect because we are indebted to sin. Our prayers will decrease in value. The minute they become a hindering to our soul welfare.

There is only one way that we will be able obtain our wealth back. We must sell off the tangible treasures of sin. It will leave us debt free, but it sometimes drains our finance in our current circumstances. At least, we will be debt free in the Lord. Then, we can attain life's true riches in our heart vault. Just like the Spencer family was able to use the tangible treasures to offset their debts once they open the vault. They returned back on the scene as one of the world's most financial and powerful family. Through prayer in Jesus' name, we will be able to return on the universe scene as one of God's son or daughter in the most loving, giving, and trustworthy, most financial, and powerful family in existence.

John 16:23(NKJV)
23 "And in that day you will ask Me nothing. Most assuredly, I say to you, whatever you ask the Father in My name He will give you.

Prayer Time

Prayer is always needed at any time of the week. We must not neglect our one-on-one conversation with our Lord. Just like it is very important to have a drink of water and inhale a fresh breath of air. It is very important to breathe the spirit of prayer in our lives.

Noonday prayer has become a part of our form of worship. We need prayer warriors, and united saints praying together at noonday services. We need saints praying together because together we can accomplish a whole lot. It doesn't matter the time that prayer is set-aside for our congregation.

Many people are traditional minded when it comes to prayer. They only pray three times a day. They only pray kneeling down or standing in church. Their prayers are repetition. It is without fruits because it is not from the heart. There is nothing wrong with praying at set times, standing, kneeling, or repetition prayers, as long as it is sincere.

Many churches have set up classes on how to pray. Some people believe that the mood has to be right before you approach God. Some of us have gotten so educated that we have lost the basic. The basic is to enjoy our time communicating with our father in prayer. Prayer is simple. It is our way of talking to our Heavenly Father. There are only two requirements to get the direct connection. We must pray from our soul. This makes our prayer sincere. We must release sin because sin hinders our connection.

Some people start arguments over terms used to describe prayer when we should be focus on praying. As a matter of fact, I hear people say, "That they talk to God, but they don't pray." I hear people say, "That they pray to God, but they don't talk." We could use praying and talking with God interchangeably. They are the same. So whether you talk or pray continue to do so from the depth of your soul. It doesn't matter the terms that we use. Both terms are a form of communicating with our Heavenly Father. Henceforth, we should share from our human embodiment of ourselves all the time.

We can pray while driving in our car. We can pray while working on our job. We can pray in school or in a jail cell. In the middle of a difficult situation, we can call on God. We don't have to be formal when we have a relationship with our Father. Just like a good earthly father if we need to talk, then God will listen. Let us break away from the formality of prayer. When we desire to talk to our Heavenly Father, let us feel free to do so. We can't let society's stipulation stop us from freely talking with our Father. We can find peace in the storm when we pray. We can find more peace, in the peaceful stage of our life when we pray.

There is no secret mystical process. There have been several books written on prayer. The world has realized the power of prayer. They have made prayer complicated. We must approach him with an honest heart. God wants us to be genuinely seeking him.

Hebrews 4:16(NKJV)

16 Let's therefore come boldly to the throne of grace, that we may obtain mercy and find grace to help in time of need.

Hebrews 10:22(NKJV)

22 let's draw near with a true heart in full assurance of faith, having our hearts sprinkled from an evil conscience and our bodies washed with pure water.

Faith

What would you do if someone told you that you could have peace in the mist of your hardships? Would you think that is too good to be true? Would you do your research in order to prove it or disprove it? Would you only believe, whatever, the person closest to you says on the matter?

We must pray and not doubt his power. We must believe that he is able to do anything, beyond what we can ever dream of. Our faith powers our prayers. By praying, we can fill the true desire of our hearts.

Hebrews 11:6(NKJV)

6 But without faith it is impossible to please Him, for he who comes to God must believe that He is, and that He is a rewarder of those who diligently seek Him.

We can have peace in our hardships. All we have to do is ask for joy and peace from God. In our personal relationship with the Father, by means of prayer, and by reading his word, we have all access to his riches. Once we have established a good measure of faith, we can ask for anything. Because we understand that everything is ours. If we have faith, trust, and obey, then we will start to unravel everything God has for us. Our expectation of God will be higher, and we will receive greater things.

Matthew 21:22(NIV)
22 If you believe, you will receive whatever you ask for in prayer."

Faith is the starting point in our journey. If we don't believe that God exist? Then we will never get pass the first checkpoint. If we only believe that God exist, but don't believe that Jesus Christ died for our sins and rose again on the third day with all power, we will never make it pass the second check point. We will be forever riding around spinning our tires in the mud. Our prayers will be like a flashlight without batteries. It has the potential to light up a dark place, but it serves no purpose without the batteries. Our faith is our batteries of life, and it creates a circuit for the current to flow. When we connect with the right amount of faith, it will heighten our prayer power. Our faith will eventually shine forth light that will produce positive results in our prayer life.

Trusting

The ultimate goal in building a relationship is to be able to trust someone. Through prayer we learn to trust our God. We build up trust with casual conversations. We learn his true characteristics, by living a life of prayer and accompanied by his word. Once our relationship with the Heavenly Father begins to grow, we begin to trust and have more confidence. We start to trust in our inner voice because we know we are being led by God. There isn't anything to problematical for us. Because God works things out in our best interests, as long as, we abide in him.

2 Corinthians 3:4-5 (NKJV)
4 And we have such trust through Christ toward God.
5 Not that we are sufficient of ourselves to think of anything as being from ourselves, but our sufficiency is from God,

Shaletha had a friend that was close to her. She knew just about everything about Nicole. They spent a lot of time together. Shaletha baked cakes for a living. One time, Shaletha had too many orders, and she asked Nicole to bake some for her. Nicole knew how to bake cakes because she watched Shaletha. Nicole made them for her family on several occasions. Shaletha didn't trust Nicole enough, so she tried to make all of the orders herself. Shaletha thought, "Nicole would drop the ball." Shaletha wore herself out and destroyed all of her orders.

We sometimes act like the Shaletha when we pray to God. We don't trust him enough to fix our problems. We try to fix them on our own because we are impatient. We can't see how God is working it out, so we try to give him a helping hand. You won't always see what goes on behind the scenes, but the finish product will attest to the truth. Every time we intervene, we annihilate our good results. We wreck our situation like a crane demolishing the wrong house.

Shaletha eventually came to her senses after crying and feeling frustrated. She called her friend. Nicole had baked her cakes to perfection and had baked extra for her family. After Shaletha explained her dilemma, Nicole willingly gave Shaletha the cakes that she made for her family. Nicole helped make more cakes for the orders. Shaletha wasted a lot of time at first by not trusting in Nicole. Shaletha wasn't worried about Nicole this time. Shaletha stayed focused on her tasks and not on the ones she assigned Nicole. In her spirit, she finally got it. Sometimes, you have to trust before you get results. Shaletha was able to complete all of her orders with the help of Nicole.

After our crying and self-disappointment, we will eventually come to our senses. We can petition the Father again in prayer. This time fully trusting in him and **letting God be God**. Once we repent, he will have compassion on his children. If we get to a point that things don't seem to be adding up, then we just have to continue to believe. In prayer, seek God's Holy Spirit, which reveals those things that are hidden to our attention. We don't have to jump in because God needs no help. We only have to trust our Heavenly Father and stay focused on the tasks assigned to us.

We have to trust that our prayers will come true. Even when, we can't see them manifesting. Some of us have to stop doubting God. It is a conflict of interest. Our Heavenly Father has seen it all because he created it all. What better person to put your trust in than the creator of life. God is the source of our being. God is the one who has our best interest at heart. Yet instead, some people put their trust in his material things. One person trust lies in money and another person trust lies in power. We put trust in relationships and friendships. Relationships are sometimes broken. Friendships are sometimes shattered. We can have an everlasting relationship when we trust God. We could build up a special personal relationship with God never known to any women or men provided that we love him. Once we fully trust God, the Holy Spirit will help us gain strength. It will also help us when we pray to him by interceding on our behalf. God is our defense lawyer on the biggest case in the world. The case file name is *Hidden Sin Unknown.*

Romans 8:26 (NIV)
26 In the same way, the Spirit helps us in our weakness. We do not know what we ought to pray for, but the Spirit himself intercedes for us through wordless groans.

Listening

During our personal conversation with the Lord, we must be prepared to listen. Listening is one of the most important parts of communication. We must tune our radio station to the right channel. When we receive static, we must continue to pray for clarity and read his word while listening for his answer. While tuning your channel, make sure you don't stop on Self Talk radio. It is a radio station that is all about self. You might have to readjust the station a couple of times. Listening to Self-Talk radio, instead of the Lord could cloud your interpretation of things.

You might have to tweak the car antenna if your frequency keeps picking up bias family stations. Most of the time, they are geared one sided. Bias family stations tend to sway toward the sides that benefit them. Beware of life's airport dead zone, where no radio station is able to connect. You must stand still but keep praying until your connection is solid once again. Once you pick back up on God's frequency, then you need to turn the radio up. Uncover your ears, so you can listen with clarity.

He has always been very near us. He just waits for us to shed a couple of sin pounds before we can receive his voice.

Many people love to talk but very few love to listen. When we listen in silence, we can hear God's voice. It could be comforting to us, chastising us, or revealing things we prayed for to our attention. We just have to listen. Sometimes we have to block life out and concentrate on God. With God as our center point, we can be more acceptable to God's voice.

Many people wonder why God allows us to make mistakes. The truth of the matter is he warns us, but we don't listen. Just like a mother tells her child the stove is hot. "Please don't touch it", says the mother. He will touch it anyway because of his curiosity. Sometimes our curiosity could get us in trouble. We are naturally wired up to be curious. We have to safeguard ourselves against curiosity and listen to our Father good advice.

Proverbs 1:32-33 (NKJV)
32 For the turning away of the simple will slay them,
And the complacency of fools will destroy them;
33 But whoever listens to me will dwell safely,
And will be secure, without fear of evil."

Proverbs 19:20-21 (NKJV)
20 Listen to counsel and receive instruction,
That you may be wise in your latter days.
21 There are many plans in a man's heart,
Nevertheless the Lord's counsel—that will stand.

Answers

Sometimes when we listen to God, we will get our answer through people. We can be praying for something, and then all of a sudden somebody out of the blue starts talking to us about the same subject we have prayed on. They not only talk to us about the same subject, but they might be the one delivering to us what we asked for. Our Heavenly Father still answers our prayers. They become the carrier of his good deeds.

If we pay close attention to him, we can find his voice within the scriptures. We have been soul searching for the answers to a puzzling question and no one else could give us the answers. We prayed about it. After we prayed, then we open the bible to search for the answers. Suddenly our eyes picked up on the right verse concerning our problems. Why? Because we were in tune with God, we felt his word lifting up from the scriptures touching our hearts. Our Heavenly Father will send us the answer when we pray sincerely. We just have to clean the wax of sin out of our ears and listen.

God also send us answers to our prayers and reveals things to us as dreams or visions. We have to be in harmony with the Father to understand the message. It could be a warning or an answer to something that we had uncertainty about. Life is full of difficulty. We are fortunate to have a Father with all resolutions on any matter. This is why prayer is so powerful! We have access to the architect of our existence very near to us in prayer. We can search out God's plan for our life, realize his omnipotent and omniscient, uncover his love, notice his goodness, and locate our spirituality.

Psalm 65:5-6 (NKJV)

5 By awesome deeds in righteousness You will answer us,
O God of our salvation,
You who are the confidence of all the ends of the earth,
And of the far-off seas;
6 Who established the mountains by His strength,
Being clothed with power

Being Silent

God revealed to a man that he would receive a new car in his spirit. Pops was so excited! Pops got on the phone and called up everyone he knows. One person thought, "He is just a big show-off." The other person thought, "He got all that money and won't even help me while I'm struggling." The third person thought, "He is always bragging and prideful." No one was happy for Pops because they couldn't understand why. They thought, "Pops always got blessed because he was lucky." They never fully understood the concept. How to build a personal relationship with God? However, they thought, "They had a strong personal relationship with God." That is why when Pops told them, they were always bitter toward him. Even in time past, Pops thought," It was hard to get anyone excited about how God was blessings him. Yet instill, his excitement made him want to tell someone anyway. Pops knew that he wasn't lucky, but God's blessings flowed down upon him.

The moment, God has revealed something in our spirit to us. After we have prayed about, it is hard to keep quiet about it. We want to chatter on and on because we are excited. We are excited about what God has done for us. We are excited about what God is going to do for us. When God has shown us, how he will bless us. People won't understand. They will work against us. They can't stop our blessings, but they try to hinder the process. Sometimes we have to know how to be quiet. Ecclesiastes said, "There is a time for everything." We can ask our Heavenly Father to control our lips in this situation. We can also ask our Heavenly Father for people in our lives who can rejoice when we are blessed. It is one of prayer benefits to be able to receive God's blessings. We receive them not because we ask him for them. Our Father is a giver of good gifts. As humans, we want to tell somebody. We want to share how God blessed our lives like Pops wanted to share how God blessed his life.

Ecclesiastes 3:7 (NKJV)
7 A time to tear,
And a time to sew;
A time to keep silence,
And a time to speak;

Patience

There are two parts to prayer. Number one you must believe in, whatever, you ask for. Number two you must be willing to wait for it to come to pass. Most of the time, we believe but expect a quick turnaround. We are so impatient. We are like a bank investor trying to make quick money. The only return that we see is a quick turnaround. A person who prays must be equally good in waiting. Your waiting could be the next minute, 30 years, or more depending on God's timing. I will guarantee that it will be well worth the wait. God is beyond time. That is why we can't pinpoint a fixed time on when his blessings will take place in our life. The apostles told us to pray without ceasing in one of their many examples. We have to keep on believing, hoping, and praying without ceasing until it comes to pass.

Philippians 4:6(NIV)
6 Do not be anxious about anything, but in every situation, by prayer and petition, with thanksgiving, present your requests to God.

A man prayed for a wife. He was sure that he met his wife. He prayed to God, and it was confirmed. He couldn't see pass her many faults during the dating process. He lacked patience because the woman had many issues. He wasn't willing to work through them with her. Therefore, he lost out on his God given wife. He ended up marrying someone else. Who he thought had it together. After a year of being married, his marriage started falling apart. He asked God. Why, "did this happen to him?" The Lord replied, "I gave you a wife, but you chose free will. You decided to marry, who you wanted to marry." The man replied, "I thought, she wasn't the one for me. We were complete opposite." God replied, "The woman that I chose was rough around the edges. But through prayer and working together, before your wedding date, she would have been perfect for you. She had the right ingredients, which was faith in me and a pure heart. You didn't have the patience for me to make her into the perfect wife for you. You couldn't see the plan that I had for you. You missed out on the wife that I chose for you."

We settle for counterfeit when we don't wait on God. We have to be in tune with our inner voice. We must know who is speaking to us. When God speaks to us, we must listen. In order to be tune in, we must be in constant communication with the Heavenly Father through prayer. We must not neglect his voice like the man who was praying for a wife from God. Once our patience frequency is adjusted in, then we become in tune with God. When we become in tune with God, we will always look forward to the next day. While keeping in mind, that God grants us a peace that surpasses all understanding.

If we get impatient and move without God, we are in for a world of trouble. The minute we stop walking under God's favor and covering trouble starts. The moment we walk after self-preservation with eagerness, and then the storm of life will consume us. The moment we stop being patient then raindrops begin to fall. It seems to always rain when we leave the umbrella at home. Without our umbrella, the raindrops continually pour down on our heads until we are soaked.

The quickest way to fall, in life is to follow our own rules. In other words, we are impatient. Even though, we are impatient from birth. We cried when we were babies for our favorite toy. Not because it was a need. We were too impatient to wait on someone to give it to us. We slowly learned patience when our mother let us cry for a while for the things we wanted. We slowly learn patience when asking the Father for things when we don't receive them right away. We also learn patience after we made it through a situation with God's help. This causes us to wait on God to fix our problems.

Patience is one of prayer's jewels. When we ask God for it, get prepared to go through something. It is like searching for a lost treasure. You must first find a treasure map. Our treasure map is prayer. It wouldn't be considered a treasure if it is lying around on the grass. We always want to find the treasure, but no one wants to go on the dangerous adventure or dig the hole. We pray for patience, but we don't want to go through the trials and tribulations. Our trials and tribulations will sanctify our patience. Once we receive patience, a great treasure we have found. This treasure will sustain us in our hard times because we can reach for it to comfort our soul. Just by knowing it will be all right in the morning, will be enough to help us carry on in life.

James 1:3-4(NKJV)
3 knowing that the testing of your faith produces patience. 4 But let patience have its perfect work, that you may be perfect and complete, lacking nothing.

Luke 21:19(NKJV)
19 By your patience possess your souls.

There were two Christian women both up in age. May and Fay never missed a Sunday service. They talked about Jesus all the time. They had the same amount of misfortune. They were having problems with their children, health, and marriages. Life had really dealt them a bad hand. It seems like they entered hardship after hardship. They were in the middle of an ocean of difficulty, with no land in sight. May was very unhappy, and her problems showed up on her face. May's attitude reflected her troublesome situation. On the other hand, the one who grabbed a hold of patience jewels demeanor was very different. Fay had an inner peace about herself. Fay attracted friendly people everywhere she went because of her joy. If she ever was down, it would be for a minute. Fay possessed something different and exciting. They were both Christian women but like night and day. Remember their circumstances were the same.

Fay understood patience, and how the fruits of the spirit operate. Fay knew what to ask for in hard times during prayer. Most Christians know about the fruits of the spirit but have no knowledge of how they work together. It is so important to pray for understanding of the Holy Scripture.

Galatians 5:22 (NIV1984)
22 But the fruit of the Spirit is love, joy, peace, patience, kindness, goodness, faithfulness,

Some people want a new home built from the ground. They want it put together overnight. We love the promise of eternity but don't want to walk the course of life with patience. In order to see the new home fully constructed, you must endure the wait. In order to obtain life eternal, you must walk with patience through the course. Rain might delay the project or problems the contractor runs into while building the house. Life's curve balls and miniature delays slow our progress down sometimes. When we rush life's mishaps, could throw us off of our course. The contractor could leave a hole in the foundation if they don't take their time. It takes time to smooth out the concrete and make sure it is filled in properly. That is why the job has to be done steadily but with patience. We must walk through life praying and having patience.

Patience is a gemstone because our walk is continually. Our walk of faith and living a righteous life requires us to have patience. In order to obtain the ultimate goal, we must have it. A Christian walk should be transforming by the minute not by week to week. We should walk boldly in the spirit night and day.

Acceptance

Talking to God is praying. Listening is to wait on the Lord for the answer. Accepting is to perform our will according to God's will. It is difficult to accept the truth, especially when it rolls off of the wrong lips with no compassion. We must be willing to accept it anyway because it is truth.

One of the essential components of communication is acceptance. We must be able to accept the truth even if we can't see obvious reasoning. Communicating with the Father is vital. Acceptance is crucial if we are to grow in the Lord. We can have a conversation with God all day long. It won't profit us anything if we don't accept his advice and do well according to it. Communication is all about talking, listening, and accepting.

What good is the brake light showing on the dashboard if we don't stop to check out the car? What good is us hearing a squeaking sound, but we don't stop? Instead of stopping, we speed up to the highest speed on the speed odometer. We will surely collide because we didn't accept the fact that something could be wrong. While driving over a period of time, the brakes will give out at any time. We will surely crash and could severely injure ourselves.

It works similar to this in prayer. We ask our Heavenly Father for a blessing or clarity. Our ears are wide open, and we are desperately seeking a blessing. After we have listened and heard his voice, then we get clarity on the matter. Sometimes the hardest part is acceptance, which this can be easier, said than done. When the results are favorable, it is easy. When the results are challenging, we don't want to acknowledge it. It is like driving a car, and we know the brake can go out at any time. We could severely injure ourselves or ruin our soul if we don't accept what God is telling us.

A Prayer for Acceptance

Lord let me have a favorable reception to your truth
Lord let me have a disposition to tolerate whatever you want me to do
Lord let be able to accept unfavorable or favorable peoples and situations
Lord let me always accept your advice
Only if you give me wisdom
I will be able to accept your answers because it will save my life

Asking Questions

A man was a five-star mechanic. "Junior knew everything about fixing cars", his loving wife Tamika thought. Everyone came to him to fix some of the hardest problems. Junior almost never had complaints. When Junior did make a mistake, he made sure the customer was satisfied.

His wife had a broken-down car in the driveway. "Her husband had the knowledge to fix it", Tamika implied in her mind. She knew her husband was a five-star mechanic. Tamika thought, "What good was this if Junior didn't use his knowledge to fix her car." She can't apply his knowledge to her situation. Tamika murmured, "If she could fix it, then it will be fixed by now."

Like people who know someone that knows about the bible. They can quote every scripture by memory. They can give the best answer in bible debates. There are some committees who push the truth to their members. Not to say, it is wrong or right but what if they misinterpret the scripture. We will never know if we don't do outside research for ourselves. This is why; it is vital to pray for knowledge of the truth and understanding of the truth from the Lord. Committees and people can flood us with questions and answers.

In instance, when we only read the material from their perspective, as a result, we will never look at it from the truth perspective. Our mind will only bring into memory what it learns. This can be untruth but disguise as the real truth. That is why it so very important to pray for the truth. So if what we are been presented with is not the truth, then we will know. Just like the wife thought, "what good is someone else knowledge if it doesn't help us." Tamika's knowledge of fixing cars was limited because her husband showed her only the basics.

We have to study the scripture and pray. Spending time with the Heavenly Father is the best way to build a personal relationship with the Father. Anybody can read the word in the bible and without understanding then form their opinion. We have to pray before reading and ask for understanding. The best way to learn is ask questions. Tamika could have asked her husband, "why he hasn't fixed her car yet." She just formed her opinion off of her observation. Her judgment led her to believe that Junior was capable to do just about any job dealing with cars. We tend to take this same approach with religion. We have to ask God to get a real understanding of the truth.

Tamika continually thought, "She would have fixed it herself because it benefits her interest." It is in our best interest to get to know the Father.

Quite a lot of people don't know what is in their best interest. If we know the truth, then we can live it. Instead of living through a person or committees, who might not know the truth as well as we thought they did. We have to ask questions? The Lord will provide us with the answers to our questions.

Tamika finally asked her husband the question, "Why he didn't fix her car." Junior replied, "He had never worked on a car like hers." He could have tried to fix it but probably would have destroyed her motor. Junior was waiting on another mechanic friend to get caught up with his work. Before, he has it towed to his friend shop for repair.

That is why. We can't trust in other people or a committee to deliver the truth all the time. Some people aren't that honest and will pretend to know it all. After we leave their shop, we will be rolling smooth for about a mile. Then the motor will fall out of the car, or you will hear a knocking sound just before the rod burst through the hood. We don't want to lose our life because we didn't seek the Lord for understanding on the truth. We can't blame other people or a committee for our lack of searching for the truth. It is up to us to build a personal relationship with the Father.

James 4:2 (NKJV)
2 You lust and do not have. You murder and covet and cannot obtain. You fight and war. Yet you do not have because you do not ask.

Doing

A billionaire keen on following directions had two sons. His sons were by his first wife. They went by their mother's maiden name Doe. The billionaire died and in his will had some specific instructions. Saul and Paul must go get their last name changed to Christian and go get a license to show that they completed the requirements. Once they signed their names the fortune was theirs. Paul followed the direction right down to the dotted line. Saul only got his name changed. Saul assumed that he didn't have to show his ID because his grandmother was the lawyer over the will. Saul figured she knew who he was and that everything would be okay. Saul didn't know that his father had a second lawyer over the trust too. She didn't know the grandmother or his sons. She only was familiar with the instructions the billionaire left behind to distribute his enormous fortune.

Saul and Paul showed up to collect the money. Paul, who did exactly what was instructed, instantly became half of a billionaire once he signed on the dotted line. Saul signed the paper but only did what was convenient for him to do. Saul eagerly waited for his enormous fortune, but he only received five dollars. The money defaulted to his children because he didn't follow the precise directions. Saul was too impatient and didn't even read the fine print. It stated you must follow all the instructions, or you will default on the inheritance.

A lot of time, we are like the Saul. We believe, have faith, trust, pray, listen, and receive answers, but we still come up short. We are sons and daughters of the king, by birthright through his son's blood. Yet instill, we fell to follow the instructions our Father provide for us. We lose our legacy due to our unwillingness to follow precise instructions.

If Saul knew, he wasn't going to receive his fortune by him overlooking only one step; Saul would have never skipped it. Make sure you read the fine print. Our fine print is his word. Make sure you do exactly what God wants you to do in order for your deliverance. What is the use of praying for something when we don't want to do anything? If the answer we receive is unfavorable or not, we have to put forth an effort when it is call for an effort on our part.

In my car, I can enjoy a long nice ride out of town. If I never put enough gas in my car, I will never get out of Memphis. When I take the initiative to put enough gas in the tank then I can enjoy the ride. We can enjoy blessings through prayer only if we take the proper initiative to make God's plan work in our lives. The bottom line is doing nothing leads to nothing when it requires something. In order to achieve something, you must do something when it requires something.

James 2:26 (NKJV)
26 For as the body without the spirit is dead, so faith without works is dead also.

A Prayer for Doing Something

Lord let me do something
When it requires for me to do something
Let me do exactly what you want me to do
Right down to the fine print
I don't want to undo
Your plan for my life by not listening
Keep your covering over me
Let me only sit still when it requires for me too
Let my will follow your will exactly
Give me the strength to accept unfavorable answers
Give me the courage to pursue unfavorable and
favorable answers
When I receive your answer to my questions
Through prayers

Stop Worrying

One the common phrase is, "I gave it to God." Giving the problems to God is easier say than done. We tend to give our problems in prayer to God but take it right back after we finish praying. Some people take it right back after their expectations of speedily results are rocked. Some people bring it to God in prayer and never feel a moment of release because it is wedged in their hearts. Instead of finding comfort in God's peace, they find discomfort in anxiety. Some people are sounding the alarm but muffling the entire Emergency Broadcast System.

It is a given that a mother's love is deeper than most. A mother had a son that got into an accident. Debra prayed to God to heal her son, but Debra still worried night and day. Let me give you a backdrop on the son's condition. He fell out of a tree and was in a coma. Debra prayed and prayed, but she worried and worried. Debra lost herself in her many worries. Debra fell out because of anxiety. She had a nervous breakdown. Her son recovered the next day. Only if she would have prayed and let go, Debra would have enjoyed her son full recovery. Now her son was by her bedside praying for his mother's recovery. Her son prayed and prayed, but he didn't worry. He let God perform a miracle on his mother. After a year, they enjoyed each other company again.

We have to pray and let go because worrying can destroy us. We must know that there is a difference in praying for the situation to get better each day, rather than thinking about the situation everyday hoping it will get better. The combination of the two can be deadly as well. Let us not get it confused with knowing it will get better because of our faith in God. We must know for a fact, after we prayed about it that it is already done. It is very easy to get caught off guard like Debra if we don't pay close attention. We will block our prayers every time because worrying damages our faith. If we always worry after we pray, do we truly believe it will come to pass?

I woke up one morning, and my car wouldn't crank. It appeared that the battery was okay because my inside lights and headlights came on. They were bright as normal. I would have never known that it was the battery by the appearance. I had this experience before now, so I knew it was my battery. Even though my terminal posts were connected, yet instill it only gave off a little fire. This little fire was enough to make things appear like the battery was performing well.

Like Debra some of us pray all the time and we appear to be fine. By our outer appearance, it seems we have not a worry in the world. We smile, laugh, and joke like normal but deep down inside we harbor worry like Debra. Only the person with similar experiences would know your stress. Our Father knows every time, so we can't fool him. Our modest expressions (little fire) that dupe our friends will not work with God. We **must stop all worrying** after we give our problems to our Heavenly Father in prayer.

Worrying Prayer

Good Father, I thank you
I honor you
I seek you
I thank you
I rest my worries upon you
I'm letting go now
If I don't know, how to let go
Heavenly Father, show me how to let go
Let me leave my burdens with you

In the past, it has been hard for me to do
I claimed that I am worry-free
You knew all the time after I prayed to you
I took the worries with me
I pray for a release
I pray that I truly leave my worries with thee
Father, take away my problems
That causes stress, pressure, and anxiety
Let no nervous tension remain
I ask in Jesus Christ name

Luke 12:22-28 (NKJV)

22 Then He said to His disciples, "Therefore I say to you, do not worry about your life, what you will eat; nor about the body, what you will put on. 23 Life is more than food, and the body is more than clothing. 24 Consider the ravens, for they neither sow nor reap, which have neither storehouse nor barn; and God feeds them. Of how much more value are you than the birds? 25 And which of you by worrying can add one cubit to his stature? 26 If you then are not able to do the least, why are you anxious for the rest? 27 Consider the lilies, how they grow: they neither toil nor spin; and yet I say to you, even Solomon in all his glory was not arrayed like one of these. 28 If then God so clothes the grass, which today is in the field and tomorrow is thrown into the oven, how much more will He clothe you, O you of little faith?

Chapter 2 Knowing more about Prayer

God's Will

John 5:14-15 (NKJV)
14 Now this is the confidence that we have in Him, that if we ask anything according to His will, He hears us.
15 And if we know that He hears us, whatever we ask, we know that we have the petitions that we have asked of Him.

Quite a few people pray and say if it is God's will. They don't fully understand the concept of the ideal. They want God's will to be done, but they want their will to be put first. Sometimes when we pray like this, it will be a conflict of interest to what we really want. Majority of the times, it is just empty words that are spoken by the person that doesn't comprehend the deeper meaning. I call these words, Filler words, for the person who prays and doesn't really understand. God's will a lot of the times takes us off the road we are traveling on which was smooth and easy. We may land on a road with bumps, potholes, and rocks. But with the right mindset, we can still find some of the comfort of the easy road. That comfort that we could find is in God's will and we could get it by asking him for peace. God will send us the comforter (Holy Spirit) to comfort us in our most uncomfortable moments.

Cherry faced some uncomfortable circumstances. She was a devoted woman to the Lord. Her religion was true not just a religion ritual. Cherry prayed every night for her situation to get better. It seemed like it never got better. Cherry always would say, "If it is your will, let it be done." In her going through, God would always comfort Cherry but never pulled her out of the burning fire of life. Cherry knew deep down inside because God placed that knowledge in her spirit. God was with her, and Cherry had to go through it. Cherry could have abandoned her post and went another route, but she stayed focused on the Lord's will. Cherry prayed to get pulled from her moldering flaming situations. God used her circumstances and experiences to bring many people to Christ that was the reason why he didn't honor her prayer request. Cherry truly wanted to please the Lord and God was truly pleased with her.

So be prepared if our prayers aren't lining up with God's will. We may be denied. Especially when, we ask our Father to sync our prayer requests up with his will. Jesus and Paul requests were denied because they were in the Father's will. Jesus could have called ten thousand angels, but he suffered for you and I because it was the Father's will. Paul's prayers were denied three times because he was in the Father's Will. Cherry's prayers were denied also because she was in God's will. Jehovah looks out for his whole creation.

The majority of the times, we are looking out for ourselves or people we like. Take notice, you might be the one our Father uses to deliver the message. Please don't get discouraged when your prayers aren't being answered. You might play a bigger part in the Father's plan than you think. Especially if, you are lined up with his will.

2 Corinthians 12:8 (NKJV)
8 Concerning this thing I pleaded with the Lord three times that it might depart from me.

Matthew 26:39 (NIV)
39 Going a little farther, he fell with his face to the ground and prayed, "My Father, if it is possible, may this cup be taken from me. Yet not as I will, but as you will."

Just because our prayers aren't being answered, doesn't always mean that we don't have the right motives. We might be doing everything right. Sometimes our prayer requests aren't answered because it is for the greater good of humanity. It involves a bigger part of the master plan. Sometimes our suffering is for someone else's healing. We might have to endure hardships, so God's plan is worked out in someone else's life. Just because our prayer requests aren't answered, don't give up. The end is far better than the beginning.

We have to keep on sharing with our Father. Ask him for clarity, and God will give us a clear view. Then we will be able to see the picture clearly if we are truly lined up with God. My friends have joy. Through Jesus, we can find that happy place in the middle of a war zone when we are in the Father's will. Remember Cherry was able to endure her hardships because she had God's peace and joy while doing his will.

A Prayer to be kept in God's Will

Father, preserve me in your will
Father, preserve me in your truth
Father, preserve me in your love
Father, preserve me in your wisdom
Father, preserve me in your knowledge
Father, preserve me in your light
I don't want to follow my will
Your will is wisdom, power, and truth
Father, preserve me in your perfect will
Then I shall truly live

Religion Rituals

Religion has become so institutionalized that true worship is missing. Some people are so involved with the religious service that they forget to love God, admire him, and respect him excessively. We have to set our hearts up for true worship. We may have to re-adjust our personal beliefs, values, and attitude before we can truly worship our Father. Some might say, "Why does God need our worship or prayers." He doesn't because he is the Almighty God. Many people ask the wrong questions majority of the times. The right question is, "Why do we need to worship and pray to God." Praying and worshiping to God operate on our hearts. Praying earnestly, help us accept and understand God more. In the process, we begin to understand ourselves more too. As a matter of fact, we learn from interacting with people. In like manner, we learn identically through praying to God.

Religion isn't supposed to be a straitjacket experience. If our religion runs us crazy, then we have a very big problem. Our prayer life shouldn't be a requirement to squeeze the vitality, adventure, and spontaneity right out of us. It should be refreshing, uplifting, revitalizing, and renewing to our life. Being that we truly adore God! For this reason, we should be willing to pour out our hearts to God.

In our prayers, we should find self-confidence, self-reliance, and self-assurance through our awesome experiences sharing our intimacy with God. Our Heavenly Father will astonish us with his answers. We can enjoy his presence and knowledge. By the same token, if we feel stuck, depressed, sadden, or dishearten by our religion or prayer life, then this is a cause for us to be alarmed. Granted, we gain no understanding about God or prayer meaning in straitjacket experiences.

However, some people have no structure or rigorous habits. They go with the flow. In their religion or a prayer life, they never have steadiness or sense of balance. It is all a guessing game. One week they pray on a daily basis earnestly. The following week they are lucky to pray one day in that week. Even so, other people prayer life has become a mundane duty. We must be nonnegotiable to a certain point and be serious with our prayer discipline and practices, while creating a good prayer habit. Let us not get too caught up in habits that we forget the true meaning of prayer.

Let praying become a lifestyle not a religion ritual. The idea of praying to pray because it is required, will compromise our worship. We shouldn't compromise ourselves by praying without integrity. This key point shapes up our motives with the Lord. Therefore, remember prayer is a privilege that our Father give to his children. Let us take advantage of this privilege with joy, love, and deep respect.

A Positive Mind in Prayer

Countless of people don't like to take responsibility for themselves. They are stuck in the same way of thinking. As a result of, their thinking creates their habits and ways. They consistently do the same thing over and over again. Always asking, our Father to change their situations. At the same time, they are looking desperately toward God for a miracle transformation. They were unaware that all they needed to do was, start moving. They let their negative surroundings consume them. Before progressively moving and grabbing a hold of their goals, they throw in the towel. They don't know how to positively influence their thoughts because of bad habits.

Their future was in reaching distance, although they didn't reach for it. We also can stop our own success by getting sidetracked by our negative surroundings. The moment we forget to utilize prayer as our key to success. We can get engulfed in the negativity. It is so easy to meditate on the things that weigh us down. These things in deep meditation can cause us to be depressed.

We have to get in the habit of praising God instead of worrying about things that are out of our hands. There is no reason why we should be sad all the time. No way should we think negative thoughts all the time if we truly have a personal relationship with our Father. Our positive lifestyle should be contagious. It should ignite our surroundings with enjoyment. Just knowing our joy sometimes motivates others is a good enough reason for us to stay on point. How do we stay on point? We stay on point by knowing when to battle, when to let go, when to shut up, and when to speak up. We stay on point also by steadily staying in communication with our Heavenly Father.

We must keep a positive mindset in order to meditate on our desires. Thinking negatively all the time leaves us with negative results. Negative equals negativity, so no way can we create a positive force. How can we destroy our negative mindset? We should declare things to be positive while eradicating every negative emotion. By letting a love mindset overcome a fear mindset to conquer life, we can lead a victorious life in many difficult situations. In other words, in Jesus, we have the power to tame our emotions by asking in prayer for control. God can help control our negative thoughts with positive ones. Going forward, our life should be uplifting because we gave our burdens to God in prayer.

I woke up one morning. It seemed like nothing went right. I had no minutes on my cellular phone to call anyone. I still remained positive. Once I made it to work, I discovered my tire was on flat. I chose to continue my positive mindset. Right after, I discovered someone was trying to discredit my reputation by starting rumors. I never said whether at home or at work, so you will just have to guess. I asked God, "To place the truth within the person's heart that was given the false information, so that the individual won't be led astray by those rumors." I remained positive. God let the truth shine forward within their heart.

The average person would have crumbled. To make matters worse, at the end of the day, I flushed my keys down the toilet. Oh yes! That would have been the turning point for most people. I can imagine the frustration on someone else's face if they would have had a day like mine. My house and car keys all went bye-bye. A coworker offered to lend me a jack, but he couldn't find the handle. This was enough to make me want to scream. On top of all that, my wife had to work late.

I'm normally patient. I started to feel discouraged, but I clung to Jesus. To make matters worse, I missed my ride home. Yet I didn't accept the negative, but I found comfort in Jesus. Calmness overfilled my soul. Our Heavenly Father gave me joy in a negative situation because I was unwillingly to accept the negative. My heart was filled with positive thoughts and encouragement from the Lord. Once I finally made it to my destination, I was happier than a child eating cotton candy at the Delta Fair. I walked in the house joking and laughing. If they didn't know any better, they would have thought I made the whole thing up. I had peace that could only come from God. My worst day was my best day because I was able to share it with you. Oh yes, I just so happen to be editing this portion of my book when this happened.

From my experiences, we have to stay prayed up in order to think positive. The actual minute we feel paralyzed or depressed over our life because things aren't lining up, we should start praying immediately. We must continue to express our thoughts to our Father in prayer that he might send us joy to overcome, whatever causes our hearts to be heavy.

Chapter 3 What Hinders Prayer

Why People Feel like Their Prayers Go Unanswered

I have heard a few people say, "God is always answering your prayers, but God never answers my prayers." When in theory, they never specify their generalize prayers to the specific things that they want from God. They only make broad comments like, "I wish God would bless me like you. I hope God bless me with a new car, house, job, etc…" They make those broad comments only because they are focused on your blessings instead of focused on their own blessings. In order to get what you want; you have to pray for what you want. Your prayers might go unanswered because you are counting someone else's blessings for the wrong reasons. The right reasons are that you are encouraged by other people blessings; so this gives you hope to look forward to your blessings. The wrong reasons are that you hate on people, so you count their blessings to supply a reason for yourself not to trust God.

This is one of the main reasons that people feel like their prayers go unanswered. They confuse broad comments with actually praying for what they want from God in order to receive those things.

We shouldn't make broad comments or count other people blessings. Remember God can answer our prayer requests in an instant, but if God doesn't, we have to continue to pray. We will never learn to be successful in prayer, if we try only one time then give up. We have to continue to accelerate our personal relationship with God through prayer.

When we drive a car and our foot is on the gas pedal, the car continues to move. The car will stop the minute we release our foot off the gas pedal. It might coast for a while depending on how fast we were going. When the car stops there is no more movement. Our prayer life is similar to this. When we continue to talk to our Heavenly Father, we can hear his voice. The moment we stop communicating by reading his word and obeying his voice, our hearing is weakened. We can be in a silent place, and it will still be hard for his voice to penetrate our ears.

Even though some people still ask the question why. "Why doesn't God hear my prayers?" Some people aren't listening to him in their silent place. Others may be living contrary to his love. They have so much anger built up in their heart. God can't sit upon our heart's throne because he is love. The minute we forgive from within not only from without, the line of communication grows stronger. The signal has the potential to reach farther and farther. God will give us everything our hearts desire according to our inward love.

Because We Fail to Pray

For some people, the reason why their prayers aren't answered is because they never prayed a single prayer in their lifespan. They don't believe in God. If you are one of those people who picked up this book out of curiosity or to see what I had to say, please pray the Nonbeliever's Prayer. After all, what do you have to lose?

The Nonbeliever's Prayer

God, I pray
God if you are true
Who are you?
God, I pray
Do you exist?
Are you a myth?
God, I pray
How have you been working in my life?
God give me understanding of you
Let me not be misled by any other false gods
If you really created the heaven and earth
God touch my heart
So that I can acknowledge you first
Give me insight on your love this day
Take any shackles off of my mind
So if you do exist, I will acknowledge it
That you are the God over all creation not just
humankind

Overthrowing Sin

Peter traveled from Memphis to St. Louis on a ship. At every dock, he stopped and bought every item the town was famous for. The more stuff that Peter accumulated caused his ship to run slower and slower. The trip was slated for 5 days. Peter accumulated so much stuff that his boat barely moved. Peter couldn't believe it because his boat normally moved at rapid speeds. Peter didn't pay any attention to the capacity plate on the boat when he first purchased it. We sometimes are caught up in sin and forget to look at life's capacity plate, which reads *sin destroys our life*. We sometimes accumulate a little sin here and a little sin there. Before we know it, our life is in a tailspin.

Peter just thought that his fuel gauge read wrong. He stopped at the next port for gas and more famous items. Once his gas tank overflowed, Peter thought, "I just need some oil." At the next port, he bought more items and some oil. It wasn't until his trip was delayed about 5 more extra days, then Peter realized something else could be wrong. Peter puzzled his brain because he had tried everything that he could ever think of. Peter miserably crept down the riverbank of the Mississippi.

We sometimes get caught in the same scenario, miserably walking through life. We try any and everything to try to fix our life. We lose weight, buy new homes, marry, and by new clothing trying to escape depression. We try to escape our environment, our circumstances, and old habits. We sometimes feel like Peter depressed, barely moving down the Mississippi River without a clue on how to fix his ship. Our ship is our life, which might be all broken down.

Peter grew depressed because he couldn't figure out the root of the problem. After the tenth day, he bowed down and prayed. A light bulb flicked in his mind. Peter realized that he stockpiled too much junk on his ship. Peter immediately started tossing his prize valuables but worthless possessions into the river. Peter yelled, "Thank God it is not my ship." The moment, we realize that it is not our prayers that hold us back, but the sins we hoard along the way while living. Through Jesus Christ, we learn to focus on a positive life, and he helps us peel away our sins. Our blessings are tied to a connection. We must get rid of our stockpile of sins, so our prayers can rise swiftly through the heaven returning a blessing to us.

So if we are at a point in our life when it seems as though our prayers aren't breaking through the roof of our house. We have to inventory the records of our ship and see how much worthless valuables we have. Have we accumulated hatred, jealously, lying, stealing, killing, talking about people, always putting people down, non- loving, non- sharing, not listen to our parents, always negative, and out for self etc...? Then immediately, we must start tossing them overboard. If we don't get rid of what is holding us down, the problem will still exist. No matter how hard we pray and try to fix a matter. Our sins have to decrease before our blessings increase. After Peter overthrew enough of his dead weight his ship started moving at a record pace. Once we remove our dead weight, our life will change in a record pace from alright to doing remarkable.

The Right Motive

Some prayer requests remain unanswered because we have barriers between God and us. Our Father hears and empathizes with our prayers. We must make sure our objectives are authentic, while praying to the Lord. Our Father will accommodate all our personal wants and desires if we pray with the right intentions. Our intentions should not be self-serving but focus on the blessings of our neighbors as well. We should make our request with the right attitude when we pray for a person.

Ruth had a boyfriend. He was down on his luck. He tried to find a job. Ruth prayed to God to help him find a job. Ruth prayed the same prayer every night. She was disappointed when he didn't find a job immediately. Ruth knew the power of prayer and how it worked. Ruth was shocked. In times past, when she prayed for people seeking employment, they would receive a job offer almost within the next couple of weeks.

Ruth's motives weren't right, so her prayers were hindered. Ruth wanted him to receive a job, so he could spend all his money on her. She sort of prayed for his career, but Ruth really prayed for herself. Ruth only wanted the returns on the prayers she made. Ruth thought of just about everything that his check would be used for like furnishing her home. Her intentions weren't correct. Ruth's prayers weren't answered like in time past.

Ruth showed selfishness on her behalf. When our prayers are all about self or what can we get out of the deal, this is a big problem. We will lose every time. God judges the heart and its intentions. According to our motives, our prayers return blessings. We always have to have the right motives in order to receive some things from our Father.

John prayed for his wife Martha to live. She had a serious disease. John trusted in the Lord to deliver his wife. Not knowing, Martha was highly favored too. She requested, "That the Lord stop her suffering." So we have two, highly favored people praying different prayers. God see the intentions of their hearts. He will grant the one with the sincere motive. John's motive was, "He didn't want to be alone." Martha's motive was, "She was tired and ready to see the Lord."

John got disgusted when his prayer wasn't answered. He didn't know secretly Martha prayed to God, but her prayers were answered. After all, it was her life, and Martha had suffered enough. We have to pray for guidance, clarity, and understanding on how to pray for the right things with the right intentions. It is hard when our emotions are involved. Emotions tend to sway on the opposite side (all about self), which can lead to the wrong motive.

Forgiveness

Forgiveness is a big part of being a Christian. It is one of the most difficult things to do. It seems like when we forgive someone, they turn around and make the same mistake over and over again. We build trust houses that are burned to the ground by false promises. So many people fall short of the glory of God because they really don't truly understand forgiveness. We briefly understand the concept of forgiveness. The match that lights our flame is selfishness. We give people our heart and work hard to please them because we want that same feeling in return. We don't seek God first, but after, the flame has caught a blaze. The flame is the concentration of all I had done for this person and all of the love I have shown this person. Then soon, we see the flame starts to heat up. We heard the smoke detector but never thought to call the fire department. In life's relationships, we feel the anger but continue doing our mundane duties. Not once, do we call on God for help.

When we decide to call, we call the operator with the wrong information because we are caught up in the moment. When we call on God, we pray for what we think is the right things. When we are caught up in the moment, we pray for the wrong things that won't better our overall situation. We go for the quick fix, but the problem is deeply rooted.

When the fire chief submits his report, he discovers that we lit the matches and never blew it out. When we do a thorough investigation, we find that we do good to receive good, but never truly changing our natural nature. In order to fix the problem or put out the fire, we have to take action now. We can't let bitter feelings linger on and on. It will eventually burn down our house. Sometimes we need the fire department help when it has gotten out of control. We need God's help because he can extinguish the fire so it will never again restart.

Abigail had three daughters and one was taken at birth. The two daughters that grew up in the presence of the mother knew the mother's character. They knew Abigail would give her last to them. They knew their mother only looked out for their best interest. They knew Abigail was a loving mother that they could trust. Mary the other daughter, who grew up outside the house, will have doubts. Mary will have a hard time believing her mother was those things because Mary grew up apart from Abigail. It will be even harder for Mary to believe Abigail if her sisters show ill feelings toward their mother. If her sisters show ill feelings toward Abigail, Mary could reconsider getting to know her mother.

Similar to the three sisters, we as Christians and saints know our Father. We know he is love. When dealing with our brethren that is unlearned or not on the same level as us, we must teach with divine love. Always remember just because we are familiar with God's goodness, our brethren might not be. They could have been brought up in another household. We should always seek God's help in the choice of words to say to strength communication with our brethren. Non-Christians also view how we treat each other. A person will most likely get involved when they see love in the atmosphere. We have to stay prayed up, so love can bathe our atmosphere.

Gradually over time, if Mary observes the other sisters love toward each other, then she will more likely want to be a part of this flow of love. Then eventually, Mary will want to know more about her mother. It could be difficult for her at first because Mary may not understand the reason why. Mary's mind could be filled with questions about the reason she was abandon. Just like Mary, the nonbeliever or beginner Christian will want to know more about the love of God after seeing our positive outer display of affection. After the initial contact, then we can provide more insightful information about God.

In her circumstances, Mary's feelings of abandonment could make it hard for her to forgive. Mary may rationalize in her mind the reasons why over and over again. Why her life turned out this way? These set of emotions are hard for anyone to deal with alone. Anger preys at the door to overtake our emotions. Mary could become bitter and carry deep resentment toward her mother. If Mary does this, then Mary's hidden secret anger will destroy her present love. In the same way, Christian's love is destroyed over petty dispute, non-saving doctrines, and theological matters. It destroys our love because it is hidden. Even though we don't know it exists. We may think that we have settled the matter, but the issues are very much present. We must pray to dissolve any hidden issues of anger before it takes control over our life in a different form.

If Mary is consumed by anger, she could resolve the situation by releasing her anger immediately. Then, Mary can bathe in love. Even if her mother is reluctant to accept her as a daughter, Mary can be kind in and out of Abigail's presence. The reason why is Mary does it out of love and doesn't expect anything in return. Mary knows that she has to forgive if she wants God to forgive her. When we make amends, we shouldn't be expecting anything back. We should be in awe because our God forgave us of our sins. Knowing that we are surrounded by God's love, we can endure any obstacles. There is no such peace like the peace of truly forgiving someone. We can only truly forgive by praying and with help from the Holy Spirit.

We will always have some cases when passion for our fellow man isn't enough like a lost mother that doesn't want to be reunited with her daughter. In order to win that confused brethren, lost Christian, or nonbeliever, we have to petition our Heavenly Father. We can ask our Heavenly Father, how to soften the blow and help awaken their spiritual reality on forgiveness. Through prayer we might be able to win them over, that is why the bible says pray for one another. A lot of times, we will criticize one another, and we forget to pray for that person who is having a hard time forgiving. Especially if we know better, then we must do better. Talking about anyone having a hard time accepting forgiveness won't help their soul. Praying for them will help them all day long. We must pray that they understand forgiveness and that God touch their heart, so they can truly be able to forgive.

James 5:15-16(NIV)
15 And the prayer offered in faith will make the sick person well; the Lord will raise them up. If they have sinned, they will be forgiven.16 Therefore confess your sins to each other and pray for each other so that you may be healed. The prayer of a righteous person is powerful and effective.

Ephesians 6:18(NIV)
18 And pray in the Spirit on all occasions with all kinds of prayers and requests. With this in mind, be alert and always keep on praying for the entire Lord's people

Resentment

A father had a son who he loved profoundly. They were an inseparable pair. One day they had a heated argument over something small. The father told the son to never return. Both of them were heated and decided not to speak to each other again. Some time had passed, and the son found the urge to speak with his father. By that time, the loneliness of him missing his son started fluttering in his heart. The father accepted him back in the home with open arms. Their relationship was never the same. The bitterness of his son disrespecting him lingered in his heart.

We are gradually separated from the Heavenly Father because in our heart lingers bitterness. We are bitter because of our circumstances. We are bitter because our loved ones should have been there but wasn't there. We are bitter because we tried to share a special moment with someone, but no one willingly was around to be found. We are bitter because somebody misused and abused our trust. We are bitter because of an accident that shouldn't have happened, but it did. We are bitter because we felt disrespected and left alone. There are a number of reasons why people harbor bitterness toward others. It starts out small but gradually takes on a life of its own.

The father forgave his son only on the outside. The son chose to forgive his father from within. The father only accepted him back into the house because he greatly missed him. A lot of times, we accept people back in our lives because we sincerely miss their company. We are like the father because we forgive on the outside. The father thought he truly forgave his son but didn't quite understand the deeper meaning of forgiveness. We barely understand the deeper meaning ourselves. It doesn't matter how long we have been Practicing Christians. That very same bitterness drives us further away from God. If it goes unchecked, it could cost us our soul. We must release the entrenched bitter taste from underneath our psyche.

The father tried different approaches to make things as they were. It only seemed to be better, but it ripped apart at the seams. Their relationship was great at first because of the newness of them being back together again. It later began to breakdown. The father started accusing the son of stuff he didn't do. The father had good intentions. The father thought no ill will was harbored because he thought he forgave his son. Yet instill, it was hidden, slowly arising inch by inch. We tend to do the same to people when we thought we forgave them. The resentment will have us thinking people are talking about us when in fact they are not. Every effort we put forward to make our relationship work will never blossom. The hidden regrets set in coming off the back of resentment plays to our deception every time.

In order for the father to truly forgive, he must let go his regrets of how things could have played out. It is amazing how our unresolved issues haunt our future like it haunted our past. Life is full of regrets about things. We can't hold resentment toward people who disappoint us. We can't store up ugly truth because people have abused our honesty. Our words, "I forgive you" become superficial. It is merely just a phrase, which rolls off of the tongue from our lips. It is far from our heart and mind. We must release the vicious circle of resentment through prayer within the inner man. So it won't resurface in another form that is more deadly than the first. The incarnation form can kill the soul.

Prayer for Resentment

Lord forgive my debtors
Let me remember it no more
Let me harbor no more resentment
Place things where they should be
Cleanse me
Cleanse my offender
All I surrender
I want to feel new
I don't need any old baggage holding me down
I want to feel renewed
I depart ways with any resentment
Whether old or new
In Jesus name
All hidden resentment is removed too

Forgiveness of Self

In addition, another thing that hinders prayer is the unwillingness to forgive self. It is hard to escape that feeling once we realize we did something wrong. It will eat away at us. That particular moment will playback over and over again in our minds. If we a have misunderstanding among anyone, then we will feel out of place in that person's presence. This can cause us to feel out of place in God's presence. We tend to fall away because we are so consumed with guilt. We feel as though God might not accept us back in his presence because we keep on having reoccurring mishaps. Then, we turn to other measures to relieve the guilt. This bridges the gap a little wider and deepens the wound.

Instead of beating up on ourselves over and over again, we must relieve our guilt in prayer. Often times, the victim of our offense will beat up on us also, especially if they haven't forgiven us. We just have to let go and still love them no matter what. It could be under some uncomfortable conditions. Forgiving self is a part of our healing process. Each moment, we neglect to forgive self the line of communication with God freezes up. We will feel unworthy to approach him in prayer. When we pray the line of communication begins to unthaw. God will forgive us when circumstances and people won't.

We are the captains of our soul; so don't be like the captain of the ship with a little pinhole. The little pinhole in his ship won't make it sink immediately. When he neglects the pinhole over time, it gets bigger and bigger. The vessel will take in too much water and sink. We have to pray for release of our guilt before it consumes us. God has already forgiven us once we repented sincerely. We just have to release and let go. In our praying process, ask God how we can make amends with a person if we have offended anyone.

Anger

Always remember God is love. Anything that is the opposite of love is at opposition against God. Love builds us up while anger slowly destroys us. Hidden grudges eat away at your soul. Majority of the time, we can't remember why we are so bitter. It doesn't take but a minute for something so small to get blown out of proportion. Anger will easily set in. That anger leads to sin if unchecked. It is one of the deadliest things to your soul like potassium cyanide is one of the deadliest things in the world. Unchecked anger sucks the oxygen of love right out of you. Your love dies of asphyxiation due to anger depriving love of its oxygen.

How can we combat this anger that leads to sin?

We must pray with the thoughts of blessing others because we know madness hinders our prayers. Anger causes our prayers to rise but fall back to the earth. It causes our positive connection to our power source to shatter into a million pieces. We have to ask God for direction on this matter. In most cases, anger is such a common emotion that love is foreign to us. Why? Pieces of hatred and jealousy are left behind from our many unsuccessful relationships. It is so easy to be angry with a person, and it takes willpower to love. When we actually love, a part of us leave us. Therefore, our weights have been lifted. When you continue to hold anger, you add a huge amount of heaviness to your soul. Praying the right prayer can help block our thoughts against anger.

How can we pray without anger when the hurt wound is still open?

We can reflect on Christ's love for us. We can reflect on how many mistakes we made, but God forgave us. We can reflect on what God have done positive in our life. Just knowing when we release anger, God will continually bless our life more. We can reflect on his love because we don't want to be a part of anger. Most of us most definitely want our weights lifted up, so we can use this as an incentive to pray in the mist of our open wound to battle anger.

For the one who doesn't know God, you can reflect on your last inhaled breath. You can reflect on your good parents or loved ones. You can reflect on your second chance in life, or the night God saved your life. Just think about how God, kept you from dying, protected you, or helped you come out of a messy divorce. God's blessings upon your life should be enough to make you want to let go of anger. God's countless favor upon your life should make you want to be a part of his love. This should be enough fuel, so anger won't consume you. Reflecting on God's goodness helps us pray without anger when the hurt wound is still open.

Panic

A warning is to alarm us. When we are alarmed, we must do something. What will you do when the alarm sound? In most companies, there is an escape plan. You are to go to the nearest escape route when there is a fire. You have to go to the storm shelter when there is a tornado. We have a plan to follow during our life disaster when a life storm hits. Our escape plan is prayer. Depending on the situation, it might call for you to pray alone. We might have to pray collectively as a whole to break down troubling strongholds. Each warning sound from God might direct us to do something different. We will be safe if we follow his instructions. Just like our earthly disaster plans for our company is put in place for safety, likewise God's words and instructions are for our safety as well. The worse thing we can do is panic in a disaster.

If we panic, it will turn into fear. We can't let our panic turn into fear. I have seen several people afraid to trust God. Several people are too afraid to pray because they think God can't change their situation. Our Father can change any and everything. God has the power over our nature, our circumstances, our hearts, and spiritual habits. All we have to do is get God involved. If we let life anxiety take control of every life event, we will get consumed by fear. Fear is the opposite of love and a weapon of the enemy.

When things get rough, focus on God and not the obstacles in front of you. If we focus on the obstacles, fear might set in, and then we will get nervous. When nervousness takes control, we begin to doubt. The minute we doubt, we will lose the faith. The obstacles will take control of us instead of us taking control of the obstacles.

A given fact is that our Father is willing and ready to fix any troubling encounter in our life. He can change and fix the wrong in our lives by means of redirection. If we panic, we lose control. When we lose control, we lose our life. We have to stand still, pray, and stare at trouble in the face. We have the upper hand because we have God on our side. We must never fear life woes and strife. Always look to God for the answers first, instead of looking to man for the solutions first. We must seek his yes or no, not our brothers or sisters' non-biblical opinions. God's word doesn't need a modification.

However, beware because God sometimes might provide us with our answer through our brothers or sisters. We must be conscious of the means, which God uses to speak his word to us. I have seen some people miss the message intended for them because they worried about the lips God chose to deliver his message or blessing. So we have to pray to God to show us and help us listen to his answer no matter what. How it comes or who it comes from. We can't afford to panic. The instance, when we panic, everything becomes confusing. We have to relax and slow down. Praying so our Father can block out the enemy at all costs, so we won't be deceived. Remember God used a donkey to speak his word, and he used a false prophet to speak blessings over his children Israel. If he uses a liar to confirm our blessings, in our heart, we will know if it is true. Therefore, there was no modification to God's word. Yet instill, if we panic, we will not hear the true conformation from God. The liar might sell us a fib.

Repent

A lot of times, people prayers aren't answered because they don't repent. They go through life as if they never caused anyone harm. A few minutes ago, they just talked about someone. They just lied, stole, or hated on their neighbors. They pray continually, but it seems like none of their prayers are answered. They wonder why? Let the truth be told, "Their prayers are empty."

I have experienced praying an empty prayer before. An empty prayer is a prayer just said, but we surely don't mean what we said. An empty prayer is our lack of humbleness in prayer because of self-gratification or self-righteousness. We are lip singing instead of singing prayers from our heart. Remember, we must pray as our heart melody sings praise from our heart.

How can we repent if we don't know what we are repenting for?

The only way we can feel remorse is to know what we feel remorse for. A lot of times, we get in the habit of praying for repentance in general and miss the root cause. The root is what causes issues to take up again and grow. After, we chopped down the tree several time before. We have to seek the root cause and the cure to destroy the root before it grows again.

In order to stop the root from growing, we sometimes must take some responsibility for our situation. Rethink what we believe and be willing to readjust our beliefs. We can't get into the comparisons game. We sometimes make the wrong assessment because they are unrealistic. We have to quit thinking our righteousness outshines everyone else's righteousness. We must keep a realistic view while knowing that we all stand in the need of prayer. If we don't repent our sin appetite will overwhelm us.

Sin has an appetite that is unquenchable, and it internalizes our separation from God. The addictive nature separates us from a real intimate relationship with our Father.

Our prayers were answered instantaneously but now the line is drawn in the sand. We can't escape the truth. Once we realize our sins that were revealed to us after we prayed about it, then we can see the problem. It is not because we are impatiently waiting, or our instant line is lost. It is because we have sin, and we never repented. That is why we can never get on track and receive our many blessings. God will bless us, by forgiving us of our sins, healing our community, city, state, and country when we truly repent and pray to him.

2 Chronicles 7:14-15(NKJV)

14 if My people who are called by My name will humble themselves, and pray and seek My face, and turn from their wicked ways, then I will hear from heaven, and will forgive their sin and heal their land. 15 Now My eyes will be open and My ears attentive to prayer made in this place.

A Prayer for Repentance

*Lord, forgive of my sins
That is blocking my connection with you
Lord, forgive me of my unknown sins
The ones that are only known by you
Lord, forgive me of all my sins
So that my love for you
Can grow stronger
Please remember them no longer
Lord, I repent
My life is in discontent
Lord, I repent
Lord only in you
My heart can be content
Wash me through and through
Forgive me and give me the strength
So that all of my sinning, I can discontinue*

Chapter 4 Other Areas of Prayer

Love

If love is our air, then faithfulness is our oxygen. Patience, joy, and peace are our food and water. Goodness and gentleness are our shoes and clothing. We need patience because without patience, we will die from thirst. We can only go without water for so long before we get dehydrated. A Christian gets dehydrated because things aren't shaping up fast in their life. They think prayer should be instant. A person with no patience will easily turn back to their natural ways. We can live without shoes and clothing, like kindness and gentleness. In certain climates, it will make our life difficult because it is a necessity. It is a necessity if we are living as Christians. It is a reflection of our light. We will be forever miserable if we don't have God's joy and peace. It is like food because without it in our trials and tribulation our love will die. We cease to exist when we have no love. Love is the breath and the very attribute of God. It is the air that we receive in our lungs through prayer. We have to have oxygen and nitrogen to make-up the air we breathe. We have to have faith in order to love our Heavenly Father and understand his love.

We must breathe love, so we can start our walk with God. Once we walk in love towards God by continually doing his commandments then we can stand any storm. We will know we can petition him in prayer for his peace and inner joy. Even though we face some of the same problems of the world, our hearts can be at ease. We should know in patience everything shall work out for us. We can have faith in all good things even when we are having a bad experience. God is alive and sits on the throne. That is why we have to pray for love. All of God's commandments rest on love. If we possess real love, then we possess the kingdom on earth as it is in heaven. By our acquainted symptoms of his love, people will begin to see Jesus through us. People will desire to get a hold of the family trait. It transcends beyond the many cultures because it is the divine agape love of God.

God
is
Love

Once we obtain love. We obtain our breath in the spiritual man. When we breathe in love, we breathe in the Holy Spirit. A positive explosion takes place in our life when the two compounds meet. It is the positive force of God working in us. Similar to TNT, it blows up sins that hide in the core of our inner man. Without love in the compound, it will not ignite. We can light the fuse all we want too, but the explosive will be a dud. Identically, if we go to church, read scriptures, and pray without breathing in love, we are just doing something. We really are not doing anything because we haven't allowed the Holy Spirit to breathe in our life by way love. Most people are on a respiratory machine in church barely breathing because they don't have faith. They have a hard time loving their neighbor and God. Just because they refuse to allow love to flow through their lungs, therefore they can't inhale the Holy Spirit.

1 Peter 1:22-23 (NKJV)
22 Since you have purified your souls in obeying the truth through the Spirit in sincere love of the brethren, love one another fervently with a pure heart, 23 having been born again, not of corruptible seed but incorruptible, through the word of God which lives and abides forever,

How Early Prayers Affect our Current Situation

Sometimes our previous prayers prayed earlier in life, affect our current situations. Very often, we ask for something when we forgot about it, it comes to pass. In contrast, it may be causing some disruption in our present-day lives. On the positive side, those prayer requests could help us gain strength in our up-to-date spiritual walk. It all depends on what we asked for like patience or love. These fruits of the spirit normally come with time and tribulations. Even though, we thought our request was very simple. Keep in mind, the obstacles we face might be preparing us for our past prayer request to take future form.

What if we prayed for the wrong thing? This can affect our current situation as well. Our mindset could have been different a couple of years ago. At that time, we could have thought bad ideas were good ideas. However, when we realize our requests aren't lining up with our existing outlook, we should pray to God. God can realign our past requests with our future circumstances. Can you remember everything you prayed for? If so, are your earlier prayers affecting your current situation? If we can't remember, we can ask God in prayer to refresh our memory.

Shun asked for patience. She diligently asked the Lord for it. One day her life fell apart. Shun couldn't understand why because she followed the Lord. Shun prayed for relief. She wanted it quick. Shun was puzzled and a bit discouraged. Shun later realized her journey started sometime after she asked for patience. Shun thought, "She wasn't going to be able to withstand it." Shun won the race and felt encouraged when she faced another obstacle. Shun knew she had grown in patience after her trials. Shun remembered a time when she would have given up instantly.

When I first started seeking employment, I prayed, "God guide my career choices. If any job I apply for isn't right for me, then God stop me from getting it. God watch over me and guide my steps." Several years later, I prayed, "God help me back on the right spiritual track." Years went by, and I forgot about the prayers I prayed. I applied for position after position. I felt like, I couldn't advance. The answers that I was given of why I didn't receive each job weren't adding up. I knew I deserved each position because of my expertise and experiences. I eventually ended up applying for my old supervisor's position after some time passed by.

They eventually hired an external candidate. I was upset because I had to train my supervisor. What is thrilling about training someone else for a job of which you deserve? I spoke the truth without restrictions, and my anger spilled over into my facial expressions. I was extremely vocal and let upper management know how great I felt about the situation. That didn't solve my problem. As a result, bitterness lingered in my heart until I met my new supervisor. Something strange happened the first day I met my new supervisor. My spirit was compelled to engage in a discussion with my new supervisor, even though I thought in my mind, "I'm not training or helping anyone." Even though upper management might have thought, "We would go to war against each other." We started a great working relationship on day one.

My new supervisor *always stated, "I'm just here for a little while, but I don't know how long."*

One day, I acted out of my character. I was upset because I felt like I was mistreated. I was loud and discussed my frustrations with anyone who would listen. My new supervisor told me, "Get rid of your angry emotions, relax, and listen to the spirit. Be patient and fully let go of your resentment, so you can really forgive." Up unto that point, I thought, "I didn't hold any ill feelings towards anyone."

God used my new supervisor to bring me something I needed. I needed the truth because this blocked my spiritual walk. If I had received that position, I would have missed my message. Here I was thinking, "God didn't answer my prayers." He was preparing me for the journey all the time. He blocked all the previous positions (I applied for) because they were not for me. I finally understood that my earlier prayers were leading up to this moment. I realized God gave me the task of helping my new supervisor with the daily workflow and gave my new supervisor the task of giving me a dose of spiritual reality. It was perfect because we both needed each other. That was one of my turning points. So you can say, *"That little while was to help me."*

Being Specific in Prayer

We must be specific in what we pray for down to the last little detail. We must ask the Father to reveal to us our spiritual and natural down falls. We must ask for God's guidance and his Holy Spirit to lead us to do his will. Jesus said, "If you ask the Father in my name, you will receive it." Jesus set an example for us while he was on earth. Jesus prayed regularly, privately, sincerely, and specifically.

In similarity, when we ask for a sandwich from a restaurant like a cheeseburger, then we will get a cheeseburger. We won't get a ham sandwich wrapped in coleslaw. By the same token, if we don't like onions, we must tell the cashier no onions. If we don't tell the cashier no onions, then guess what we will get a cheeseburger with onions.

If what we receive, is not lining up because of what we asked for. We can still petition the Father to help us understand his plan. Please be prepared for the answer, because it might not be what we think it should be. Remember that he is God, and he can see beyond what we can see. If you are still having trouble seeing your way, then asks for clarity, understanding, and knowledge. We should pray for acceptance, so we can accept whatever the answer may be.

For comparison's sake, if our cheeseburger arrives with onions because we forgot to say no onions, then we can ask the cashier to please prepare it again. If we don't get the result we desire, we can ask for a manager. The manager may shine some light on the situation. Most good managers will have it prepared fresh for you again. In some cases, the manager will give you a clear reason why they can't prepare it again.

After acceptance, the answer might be that "God gave us exactly what we asked for." We can petition the Father to fine-tune any prayer request that we have already received. We can fine-tune our prayer requests on the go also while our prayer request is still in process. This might affect our results a little or a lot, but it depends on what adjustments we make. It also depends on if it is a part of God's will.

Likewise, the manager might tell you that you ordered the cheeseburger wrong in the first place. It isn't their fault. They could decline your request, but it depends on the management staff. The cook might prepare it again, but it may not be like the one you previously had. It was almost perfect all except the onions. They might never get it looking as juicy as the first one. You must still ask to find out if they are willing to accommodate you. We have to ask God when things don't seem to be lining up in our lives. In most cases, the manager may not even own the restaurant, but God is higher than any manager. Our Father owns everything, and he will repair or prepare our life according to his will when our prayers are specific. This will be the perfect outcome, even though we forgot to ask for no onions. Most of the times, God will still accommodate us after we redirect our change of thoughts to him in prayer. Remember that our Customer Service Feedback Line to report our grievances to God is PRAYER.

On a serious note, I prayed to God for a house. I just wanted a house. I was thrilled when my prayers were answered. I didn't pray for a low interest rate, a fixed-rate mortgage, or a house in best the condition. I didn't pray for a low monthly mortgage note, so I could have some money left over to do other things. I prayed for a house, and I got a house. It wasn't until I started to fine-tune my prayers that things started to shape up. Once I realized that I had to be specific in my prayer requests, my outcome started to become different. We can't expect to receive what we don't ask for specifically because the majority of people will try to take the credit themselves. The natural minded person would say, "The Lord sent me a house, but I talked the realtor down to get a low interest rate, a fixed-rate mortgage, and low monthly notes." Our Father already knows before we ask him for things. He just gives us what we ask for, so the natural minded person wouldn't get confused.

If you are praying for a spouse, please be specific. While in the dating process and things aren't lining up, pray to God to fine tune your situation. If we have a personal relationship with him, then our Heavenly Father will accommodate us only if it is in line with his will. We can settle for what we prayed for and got, or we can ask for some adjustments so our life can run smooth. A lot of people ride around in life with cars that haven't been tuned-up in years. The cars ride, but it barely function. We take the same approach in life when we pray. If we know that something isn't working out, we won't even ask God to see why. It may need a minor adjustment or a major adjustment, but God can get our lives to run smooth again.

Balance

When loading a truck, we must balance the load. The truck could potentially turn over if we don't balance the load. As long as the truck driver travels straight, the load might be safe. It will surely shift if he makes a sudden swerve hitting a curb while going at high speeds. The driver may lose all of the customer's valuables.

We are in danger of losing our valuables, which is our soul, when our life is unbalance. The minute the load shifts it could cause an earthquake. An earthquake in our lives will shake our life apart. Sometimes people never recover from it because they are sucked under the earth. They are closed in by too much debris. Therefore, they may never reach the surface again. On our daily walk, we must balance our life. Too much of anything is bad for us. Like the writer of Ecclesiastes said, "There is a time for everything." Life is all about choices and balance. Do you have balance in your life?

I have noticed that a lot of times our life is out of balance. We lack the necessary steadiness to follow God's plan and still delight in his beautiful earth. We lean to the right or left too much. Our life should be equally fulfilled. I have seen the person who party too much and lack the very essence of life. They lack a personal relationship with God. I have seen the person who over commits their time to the church and neglect family. They found the essence in life, which is God. They lack understanding because we were put on this earth to enjoy life in moderation. Balance is another precious jewel that we should hold dear to our heart. We should ask the Lord for perfect balance over our life. So that, we serve him first and still enjoy his beautiful earth. Stability lies in the Father. God can give us a sense of balance.

My life is in the need of balance

Father God, give me balance
Balance over my finance
Balance over my family
Balance over my prayer life
Balance over my time
Balance over my morning and night
Balance over my work
Set every inch of my being according to your perfect
balance
So, I can enjoy your presence along with the enjoyment
you have given us upon this earth

Children

Parents teach their children how to ride a bike, tie up their shoes, and cross the street. We send them to the best school for a great education. We are concerned about every aspect of our children's life. We would give them the keys to success if we knew it. We will pay the highest price to invest in our children's future.

The key to our children's future is at our fingertips. It goes unnoticed by so many parents. It is simple and free of charge. A personal conversation with God each day is the key to our children's success. It will give our children the upper hand when dealing with life. If they apply it, they will have guaranteed success. A well balance life will start to develop as they continue to hold a personal conversation with God. Our children will have a life of ambition because they will know what to ask for in prayer.

The second we start taking time to teach our children how to pray, we give them a precious gift. It is more precious than any worldly gift. It is a true investment in our children's future. When our children know God, it is more rewarding than them being an honors scholar student. This is one of those gifts that our children can reflect back too in troubled times and escape life's woes. As a parent, we know through communication we draw closer to God. When we help our children build up a personal relationship with our Father, it is no such greater joy.

Children watch their parent led by example, so please give a great example for your child to follow. Show them your willingness to trust our Heavenly Father. Pray so they can see their brave parents having a discussion with the Father.

Some parents might not know how to teach their child how to pray. They might have never prayed a prayer in their lifetime. You can begin by asking God for guidance in this area on the matter. Our Heavenly Father will enlighten you, so you can enlighten your child.

Always remember to never get frustrated with your children. Let them ask for whatever they want like a bike, toys, or new shoes. Our Heavenly Father will reward them accordingly if they obey us (their parents). They will slowly grasp a hold on prayer, and its broad concept. Our children will start praying for stuff with meaning, and this will enhance their personal relationship with God. The more time they spend in his presence, then they begin to understand our Father many attributes. Our children's bond will grow stronger because of the connection to the power source, which is the Almighty God.

God wants us (*parents and children alike*) to ask, inquire, and share our deepest thoughts with him. Jesus set a model prayer for us to follow on our daily journey.

Matthew 6:9-15(NKJV)
9 In this manner, therefore, pray:
Our Father in heaven,
Hallowed be Your name.
10 Your kingdom come.
Your will be done
On earth as it is in heaven.
11 Give us this day our daily bread.
12 And forgive us our debts,
As we forgive our debtors.
13 And do not lead us into temptation,
But deliver us from the evil one.
For Yours is the kingdom and the power and the glory
forever. Amen.

This is a prayer that we should learn and teach our children. It covers a lot of bases. The Lord's Prayer covers the basis of forgiving, following God's will, and shunning sin. It is also an acknowledgement of God's kingdom on earth and heaven while honoring God's power and glory forever. The Lord's Prayer is still very relevant because it is still exceptionally powerful today.

The Inner Voice of Prayer

In the process of making a big decision, on our career or a pivotal point in our life, we first get an adrenaline rush wanting to do more. We have the motivation to go forward. After that, we get nervous because nervousness set in. We become afraid of change. We start to view things in a negative way. Under this circumstance, we should pray for peace on the spot.

Prayer for Peace

Lord, what should I do?
How should I react?
Saturate my heart with love
Bless my lips
So I can bless others
Cover me in your peace
Help me find peace by making the right decision
Help me with this pivotal point in my life
Lord, help me connect the right dots
I pray for peace on the spot

Take away my nervousness before it set in
Keep my heart positive
As I approach this change
God, you are my power source
I ask you to guide me in Jesus' name

God's peace will come in and console us. We must prepare our heart to listen to the Holy Spirit. All the time staying focused on his will, not our own. The nervousness will try to set back in. We may have to pray again for God's peace and calmness.

Prayer for his peace & calmness

Lord, place your calmness all around me
Let me soak in your love
Here comes fear and nervousness again
I will conquer it once more
Let peace be still
Let my worry heart be filled
With your Holy Spirit overflow
Keep my subconscious focused on you
Nervousness and fear I destroy
I pray for peace in middle of this commotion
Lead me
And by your will, I stand
Though there are many obstacles
By tapping into the source, I hold the upper hand

After the nervousness and uncertainty, then comes his calmness. Pay close attention and the inner voice will follow. The inner voice will lead us in the right direction. In our interaction with God, he drops the message in our conscience. For most people who are in tune with his presence, it is equivalent to your first mind or gut feeling. It leads us away from trouble and into righteousness. It helps us with all justly decisions. We feel it in every fiber of our being.

Warnings We Receive While Tuned In

As the little girl looked into her father's eyes, Elatris grew upset because she only tried to have some simple fun. Elatris thought that her life was boring and dull. Elatris felt like her father corrected her too much because her friends did as they pleased without correction. Her father seemed to be too strict and mean. In reality, Elatris had an awesome father. Elatris didn't realize it until she got into deep trouble. Elatris said, "Only if I would have followed my father's warning, then I wouldn't be in this trouble that I am in." Elatris now knows that her father only tried to protect her and keep her safe. Elatris missed his warning because her good intentions were blocked by the excitement of participating in worldly entertainment even though she knew better.

Our Father tries to warn us as well, but a lot of times, we misread the warning. We misread the warning because we are not in tune with God. Our attention is focused in the wrong direction. We are searching for the pleasure of worldly entertainment instead of the pleasure from God. Our view is block by our wrong contemplations, but deep-rooted in our hearts we know the truth. However, we set up a religion blockage. When we don't heed our warning received through our personal conversation, it becomes meaningless. That is why it is so important to stay in touch with the Heavenly Father through prayer, so we can understand and regard his warning.

My Warning

Out of the blue, I had a dream or vision. I saw myself battling with upper management. I prayed and I understood to be strong and don't fear. I knew God would guide me. I understood that people had been praying for change, and it was on the way. It seemed strange at first because everything was going smooth for a while at work. Dreaming this dream 15 minutes before work, something had to be wrong. It was almost like a referee throwing a red flag on a winning touchdown play. I thought I had won the game. Until, I had to replay the down at the one-yard line. Imagine yourself having to carrier the ball through the whole team in order to score the winning touchdown. This is physically impossible but with God's help all things are possible.

The Dream / Vision

I was playing badminton with my supervisor. My supervisor and I had never before played any games. We were playing on opposite teams. He hit the birdies hard over the net. I noticed that the birdies only had the cork part. This made the game interesting because the plastic feathery like part makes it literally float in the air. It was almost as if we were playing darts. My spirit knew that he was playing dirty. While still dreaming, I immediately understood that on my job, my supervisor would be plotting trying get rid of me. I knew he would have quite a few people in this plot. After I woke up, I remembered that I had a teammate too. I prayed that my teammate was Jesus. I knew deep down inside my spirit that I couldn't lose.

It was almost like clockwork. It was on time. When I saw my supervisor that morning, he set his plan in motion. I had to thank God because he warned me, and I listened. I felt his presence in my spirit, and I praised him with a Hallelujah.

We went through several combats, but I trusted in God. Our Father gave me ammunition to fight back when they thought they had me pin down. I realized something too; God was teaching me too. My personal relationship with God grew. I learned the true power of praying and the power of his love. I learned to whip people with love. I learned to chastise them trying to save their soul instead of obliterating their future. There were a couple of episodes, but I raised triumph.

Some time had passed, and I had another shocking dream or vision 15 minutes before work. In this particular vision, I was defending the people. I had to change the outlook of how things were run. Therefore within my spirit, I knew God would be with me and would guide my pen and lips. I prayed and praised in the center of his powerful presence in my life. I continued to recognize his love and enjoyed my personal conversation with God.

It was true again. Being that normally, when I am nervous, I can't write well or speak well. Our Heavenly Father gave me a peace that I embraced. My pen expressed the words so crisp and clear as if I was a bestselling writer that was writing a winning novel. I later had a meeting at work, and I was a well-educated lawyer whose words embodied truth and authority. I knew God was my power, and the reason my pen wrote, and my lips spoke. I knew because I trust in him and during our talk, I asked for his help.

I beseeched the Lord in prayer later on that night. I wanted to make sure that I wasn't leading myself. I know we can read things too much and misread information given to us. I wanted to make sure that I continued on the right path. I prayed for reassurance. I asked the Lord for a second conformation the next morning. When I opened my bible, I turned to Psalm 56.

Psalm 56 (NKJV)

Be merciful to me, O God, for man would swallow me up;
Fighting all day he oppresses me.
2 My enemies would hound me all day,
For there are many who fight against me, O Most High.
3 Whenever I am afraid,
I will trust in You.
4 In God (I will praise His word),
In God I have put my trust;
I will not fear.
What can flesh do to me?
5 All day they twist my words;
All their thoughts are against me for evil.
6 They gather together,
They hide, they mark my steps,
When they lie in wait for my life.
7 Shall they escape by iniquity?
In anger cast down the peoples, O God!
8 You number my wanderings;
Put my tears into Your bottle;
Are they not in Your book?
9 When I cry out to You,
Then my enemies will turn back;
This I know, because God is for me.
10 In God (I will praise His word),
In the Lord (I will praise His word),
11 In God I have put my trust;
I will not be afraid.
What can man do to me?

12 Vows made to You are binding upon me, O God;
I will render praises to You,
13 For You have delivered my soul from death.
Have You not kept my feet from falling,
That I may walk before God
In the light of the living?

I received it in my spirit. I trusted in the Lord and let him guide my battles. It was true. Some people were collectively together on one accord to deliver the defeat blow to my face. I acted in silence and observed. I was extremely content and smiled at any encounter. I knew my war was won before the first battle even took place. I knew because of my personal relationship with our Heavenly Father. I trust him because he had delivered me numerous of times. Needless to say, that situation worked out in my favor.

Praying Together

The power of prayer is togetherness. It is stronger than any man-made fiber. You can see the sparks of power when the saints join together in prayer. It will illuminate any area while they meet with a brilliant spiritual light. God's presence rejuvenates a controlling influence over our life when we are on one accord. We are all at different points of our spiritual walk with our Father. Some of us are stronger than others. Some of us have a purer heart, which allows us to walk a little closer than others to our Father. It somewhat effects our prayers to a certain extent.

Matthew 18:19 (NIV)

19 "Again, truly I tell you that if two of you on earth agree about anything they ask for, it will be done for them by my Father in heaven.

When we pray together, we increase our chances of getting a better connection with the Father. Some of us have a stronger union on our own with the Father. Just imagine what we can do with one or two people like us praying for the same thing. We can accomplish anything when two or three are joined in Jesus' name. Our physical body moves flawlessly as a unit. On one accord, our spiritual body will move flawlessly in prayer. We will send off all type of signals when we pray as a group. Our results could be endless. There might be one person who is fervent in prayer. Their requests are speedily answered when they pray to God. They have built up such a robust relationship with the Father by disregarding sin. When we join each other in prayer, then we have just added that person petitioning the Father on our behalf.

We get that extra kick by praying together. It's uplifting to the heart because we are in fellowship with God, our brothers, and our sisters. If we pray alone, we still can have a powerful relationship with our Father. We'll just be missing out on the sister and brother experience. That is why it is good to have a church home. So we stay connected together in fellowship among saints (*sisters and brothers experience*) as well as to learn. Don't forget about the obvious, someone might be counting on our smile. They might be counting on our prayers when the congregation prays. Our voice might be the voice that carrier the congregation's prayers because we have a good standing with the Lord. It could be the whole congregation is equally gifted in praying. That's great! The more the merry in making our prayer requests known to the Father.

Prayers of the Righteous Keeps You

There were two best friends. They grew up in the rough part of town. They were friends since elementary school. They did odd jobs together and frequently ate at the same table. They were two peas in a pot. They committed crimes together and they would get caught. Episode after episode, one always would get off easier than the other. The one who thought, "Man, I can't catch a break" really didn't understand. Popeye thought, "He was the unluckiest guy in the world." The other friend Renzo thought, "He was lucky in the presence of his best friend."

Neither one of them never knew, that the unlucky one mother was a righteous woman with good intentions. Popeye only thought his mother was just alright because she went to church. Popeye's mother prayed every night and morning for the Lord to help her son. The Lord had a covering over him. God shielded and protected him daily. Popeye knew his mother prayed for him, but he actually didn't know the power of prayer and how it works.

Proverbs 3:12 (NIV)
*12 because the Lord disciplines those he loves,
as a father the son he delights in.*

1 Peter 3:12 (NKJV)
*For the eyes of the LORD are on the righteous, And His
ears are open to their prayers; But the face of the LORD
is against those who do evil."*

The unlucky one was in fact the most blessed one. Popeye always got caught and punished because our Heavenly Father corrects his children. The correction he gives us is to protect us from future mistakes. It is our reminder if I do this that might happen. If some people don't have the same reminder, they continue to do the same thing over again without the fear of the Lord. Their conscience becomes dead, and self takes control. The friend with the worst luck (at least Popeye thought) conscience remains effective because he knows he can't get away with anything.

By his mother having a personal relationship with our Father, Popeye was covered. God allows him an opportunity to get right and closer to him. Our Father knows if we can get by with sin then we will continue to participate willingly. God always looks out for his children. Our Father honors the prayers of the righteous with his great power. A lot of us may wonder how we got this far. It is because of our Father's protection. It is because of the prayers of the righteousness, which prays over our life. Most of us are able to stand and come into the knowledge of the truth through Jesus Christ. We are able to overcome our worst situations.

When we understand the power of prayer, we have to pick up the mantle of prayer like the mother who always prays for her son. Let us start praying over our loved ones, spouse, and anyone we see going astray. We should ask God to cover them, so they may come into the knowledge of truth. So they might overcome their appalling situations. It is our obligation not out of duty but out of love to carry mantle of prayer. Remember someone did it for us, whether we knew about it or not. Let us keep our children, as well as our neighbor's children in our prayers, so that our Father can renew and uplift them to him. We know truly that we have no righteousness on our own, but we have pure righteousness through Christ Jesus. Our righteousness through Christ might keep them, like someone else righteousness through Christ keep some of us. You never know who is praying for you in their daily prayers to God.

Prayer Changes Things

A man was driving a car. William hit another car and damaged it. William was drunk as a fish. When William sobered up, he had remorse. He asked God for forgiveness and prayed for things to work out in his favor. The owner of the other car didn't press charges, but only asked that his car be repaired. William was saved from going to jail through prayer.

A young girl committed a crime that landed her in jail for life. Stine discovered the power of prayer. All of a sudden, she became a prayer warrior in the prison. Stine prayed for people on the outside to be healed, and she prayed for the inmates to be healed in prison when some were down on their luck. Stine prayed for herself to get an earlier release date from prison. Even though Stine was never granted that earlier release date, she became content because God touched her heart. Stine was in prison but not confined in prison of her mind. Our Heavenly Father released her with peace as she paid her debt for the crime she had committed.

A hurricane came through a city with very high winds. It damaged cars and destroyed houses. Most people were left helpless. In the commotion, a lady prayed to God in the middle of the street. Jeanette knew prayer changes things. She prayed that her car and house be spared along with her life. Jeanette's prayer didn't save her house and car, but her life was spared. Jeanette continued to pray and poured out her feelings to God. Our Heavenly Father gave her the strength to pick up the pieces and move on. Jeanette realized the strength of acceptance through her prayers to God.

We still might bear the scars from our mistake by being disobedient. Our physical circumstance might not change when we pray yet instill prayer will change our original nature. There are two ways prayer can change things. It can change things in a natural sense or spiritual sense. Prayer also can affect us in both ways.

In the young girl's case, prayer changed her in a spiritual sense. Stine still had to live with her consequences. She underwent a change of heart. God gave her the strength to press forward. Stine found hope in God, which gave her new results.

In Jeanette's case, prayer changed things in the natural and spiritual sense. Her life was spared from the storm. Prayer changed the condition of her mind. We may tend to think negative of every situation. Prayer gives us the peace to be positive in a negative situation. Jeanette was able to transform because God gave her what she needed to change. Prayer gave her a difference in essence. Our Heavenly Father gives us the central meaning of the issues we pray for in our prayer request. It can help us improve our situations.

In William's case, prayer changed his natural circumstance. William didn't go to jail, and he had another chance to make amends. The backdrop to his story was he was in tune with God. William's life reflected his walk with God because he obeyed God. He was drunk because someone spiked the punch. William realized it after he couldn't stop his car in time.

Prayer helps us get in sync with God's will. Many people underestimate the power of prayer. They would rather for prayer to play the background instead of the foreground because they think you should do more than pray. This is true to a certain extent, but prayer gets the heart prepared for the doing. We might have to cut a few things loose before we actually see the change. I'm a witness that prayer does change things. Some people changes through prayer can be seen physically while other people changes can't be seen. It can't be seen because it is spiritual.

Please don't deemphasize the fact by saying, "Prayer is less important." Prayer jump-starts the love for your brother. How will you know how to love your brother if you don't ask? How would you know how to love God if you don't ask? How will you know how to pick up the pieces in life if you don't ask? Do you see the important of prayer? If you don't talk with God, then your love for your brother might be incorrect. If you don't talk to God, then you will never learn how to accept things as they are. Prayer changes our attributes and helps us deal with our temperament.

In light of things, prayer truly changes things. Whether, you believe it or not. Sometimes prayer changes things without any manual effort, but in other instances we have to put forth a manual effort. If we seek spiritual things, then we only have to believe. God will answer our prayer and enlighten our understanding if we are heartfelt. If we seek natural things, then we might have to do some work to get the results we want. Each scenario is different, but it is according to how God sees fit. If prayer doesn't seem to change anything else in your life, at most you should acknowledge all your changes are possible through God. Once you know this you can be self- motivated and possess great self-esteem through Christ Jesus.

Continue in Prayer

A young lady left her hometown of Memphis at the age of seventeen. Linda never thought to continue her relationship with her foster mother after Linda went off to college. Linda wasn't belittled or condemned as a child. In reality, she was loved dearly. Her foster mother never understood why Linda left and never came back. After all, the foster mother helped Linda transform her life. Before her foster mom took her in, Linda never thought about finishing high school let alone college. Her little girl had now blossomed into a grown woman. The young lady felt like she didn't need her foster mom anymore. Linda thought, "I could make it on my own." At that time in her life everything was going fantastic.

Her foster mom remembered that her daughter use to cry throughout the night. The foster mom remembered comforting her daughter after her biological mother abandoned her. Oh how much great love she has for Linda her only daughter and only child. The foster mother kept her little one in her prayers. Sometimes once people have been transformed out of the jaws of defeat, their prayer life becomes unstable. It was initially steady because they tried to reach their breakthrough.

They were trying to breakthrough a bad marriage, broken hearts, awful career choices etc., so they gave God their time wholehearted. Some people are like the young lady because we confess our love in a time of need. God listens like the foster mom listened to Linda confess her love toward her every day before she left for college.

The old saying is, "In a crisis people come to God, but once they obtain stability, they forget God." One of life's essentials is to stay connected to the Father by praying which expands the line of communication. We should exercise our prayer muscle to continue to look at life through God's viewpoint. We must give consideration to how God made a way for us. We have to keep him in our sight at all times. If we don't keep him in our sight, we will forget him like Linda forgot about her foster mom.

The foster daughter eventually ran into a crisis. Linda reconnected back with her foster mom. Linda knew that her foster mom would always give her emotional and monetary support. After this last episode, she stayed connected with her foster mom. Linda felt bad because she disappointed her foster mom and never took consideration for her mom's feelings. She finally got it. The positive result that compelled her to better herself was through her foster mom's support. Her foster mom's support encouraged her to beat the odds and rise above economic and social circumstances.

The young lady was inspired by her foster mom because her spirit was enlightened. Linda knew that it was through her foster mother's diligent prayers that gave her empowerment to be delivered. She now understood the beauty of their relationship. The young lady kept her eyes on God 1st and 2nd on her foster mom of which strengthen their mother and daughter bond.

Some people are reconnected to God again after a crisis. In much ways like the young lady, it took a crisis to bring her back closer to her foster mom. It might take a crisis to bring some people back to God. Why? Once God has elevated some of us, we forget the elevator. We keep our eyes on a one-time victory. We forget because God have delivered us out of whatever situation that held us bound. We must remember just as Linda remembered to reach out to her foster mom. We have to reach out to God. We have to keep on praying, reading, and attending fellowship with the congregation of saints. It might be the congregation who help you achieve your breakthrough. Once we realize like Linda, that we still have more challenges and more conquests, and then we can keep our eyes on God not a onetime victory.

We must understand by building a personal relationship with God, he and only he could get us to a happy point in our life. We can't lose focus, but we have to keep his principles so we can continue to flourish. As your soul become harmonious through praying to our Father, we can realize our blessings. It can be so easy to forget from whom the blessing is coming from. If we don't continue to have faith, trust, and pray to him, we will lose sight every time our life is going well. We will not be any better than the young lady. The minute Linda gained stability in her life afterwards, she forgot all about her foster mom. Once the young lady comprehended on the natural side, she recognized her life's success was owed to her mother. We owe our life's success and life to God. Whether God at this moment is bringing us through a storm or we are on a beach enjoying the sun, we must continue to pray to him. For we know life's mishaps can occur all of a sudden, but we are eagerly prepared in Jesus.

The Sinner's Prayer

Imagine yourself stranded in an ocean. The chopping waves roars. All you can see is an endless ocean of water. Things seem hopeless and you breathe a sigh of defeat. When you see a rescue helicopter, you breathe a sigh of relief. The fact of knowing that you are about to be rescued is priceless.

The minute the rescue team lower down the basket attached with the harness into the ocean, the weight of hopelessness starts to fade. Once your harness is attached and you are placed securely in the basket, your nightmare is almost over. You must hold on tight, or the 20 feet waves could force you back into the ocean. You must grip the rope like you have never gripped it before. The rescue worker straps you up before he signals his other team member to raise you out of the water.

Most sinner prayers are our rescue team putting us in the rescue basket. It conditions our minds to accept God's free salvation. Just like the rope is attached to a basket and safety harness, most sinner prayers put you in a position to be pulled toward safety. We have free will; therefore God won't interfere with our will. He won't force himself upon us. He is a just God, so to force someone to love him is out of his character.

Once we accept his salvation then it opens our free will up, so he can start to move spiritually in our lives. The sinner's prayer may be the first step to show that we love him for some and is willingly to involve him in our life.

For some people, just because you say or said a sinner's prayer doesn't mean that you are saved. Some people lip just drop to the floor because that is what a lot of pastors say. *You can say a sinner's prayer and don't mean a word you said.* Were your intentions right the minute you placed your life in the rescue basket of life? If your heart wasn't right, then the ocean swallowed you up the minute the rescue team put you in the basket. The sinner's prayer doesn't save you, but it puts you in the rescue basket.

Being saved is the safety harness that pulls you up when you fall out of the basket. Jesus Christ is the rope. You have to acknowledge Jesus as Savoir and Christ and the Son of the Living God. You must believe he died but rose again with all power. Then you will get placed in the rescue basket, and your harness will be fastened as Christ begins to lift you up out of the ocean of life.

I hear people say, "Once you are saved you are always saved." Being saved is a journey. At any time during life's terrible storm, many chopping 20 feet waves can make you lose your grip. You may fall back into life's vast ocean. You are already strapped in with your safety harness and all you have to do is repent. Then you can get lifted back up with the rope of Jesus.

Just like the harness on the basket that a rescue team uses if a roaring ocean wave takes you under, you still can get lifted up to safety. Once you are saved, you are always saved isn't true. You have a safety harness of which at any time you can turn your life around. You can be saved out of life's ice chilly ocean. Being saved is a life connected to a harness with a rope, which Jesus Christ keeps pulling us upward.

A prayer to get you in the rescue basket

Lord, change my life
Lead me to the cross
Father, I believe in your son Jesus Christ
I believe he is the key to my life
I believe he rose from the dead with life
With all power in his hand
Clean me up
Help me walk this race so I can be saved
I repent of all past sin
Lord, help me sin no more
Help me learn to love
Separate my will
With your love refill
So I may desire to walk in your will
Change my heart
Wash me this moment
So you can sit on the throne of my heart

Recipe for Life

Many people think prayer is a lot of fluff, and there is no truth in it. People say, "It is only for the people that believe in junk. They don't know what they believe because the **religious** people are hypnotized by the pastors. Every day they can't be happy and filled with joy." They think we are lying through our teeth. They just don't know the recipe. I can attempt to make chocolate cookies with corn meal, but they won't be considered chocolate cookies. They might have chocolate chips in them, but it doesn't mean that they taste like your good old mother's chocolate cookies.

I hit this same wall myself wondering does prayer really work. In the course of me trying to complete this book, my family life was hitting potholes after potholes. At one time, I thought that I was stuck in a sinkhole. I knew the answer was prayer, so each event didn't deter my peace. I can recall one day when my life spun around in a split second. I got the notice that we all dread to get as a homeowner. My peace hit the floor! I lost my peace and joy for that moment.

On top of that, I was still dealing with issues on my job. Prayer at that moment didn't seem like the solution. It seemed like prayer was a lot of fluff because nothing was going right. Yes, I was discouraged. I knew how prayer works. I have seen it in action several times before. I had another moment when I opened the second letter from my bank. They charged me thirty-five dollars for an overdraft fee. I thought I had enough money in the bank to cover that purchase. My emotions ran high, and I reached another low point. I got frustrated, and the enemy started attacking. It took me awhile, but I eventually used my recipe for life. I started praying and asking for peace from God to help lead me through my situation. He gave me peace that next minute, but it was times when I had to pray through the night. The next morning everything was all right because I had a fresh different perspective on life.

We too go through changes in life because change is constant. The only difference is you see us (*Christian people who understand prayer*) smiling all the time. The reason is we follow the recipe of prayer to obtain our peace and joy before the enemy takes controls. We hurt and have pain along with life's disappointments just like everybody else. The difference is most people use the wrong ingredients but want the same results. If you want your cookies to come out right, then you must use the correct ingredients.

You can argue that corn meal instead of flour makes the best chocolate cookies especially if you never made them or taste one made of corn meal. Just like non-believers who don't believe in prayer might make a case against it. Non-believers make their case because they never tried it before, or they don't have enough faith.

If you are cursing, drinking, fussing, smoking, or using drugs in order to make yourself feel happy, then you are using the wrong ingredients. That is why you can't truly be happy. You might be using them to escape life's woes. You have strayed away from the original recipe. I have put together some recipes on different issues we face in our day-to-day walk in life starting on page 277. You can concentrate and focus on each prayer recipe for your situation. Remember, faith and obeying God are our main ingredients in the recipe of prayer. Other ingredients are listening, asking questions, and patience. All of our ingredients must line-up, so we can smile through life's turmoil. Once our prayer recipe is mixed correctly then we can enjoy the finish results. Some of the finish results are peace, comfort, and love.

The Recipe

Lord don't let me shy away
From the recipe of life
Let me keep you near
For you are the keeper of my life
I can see clearer
I need your presence close to me
I'm on shaky ground
Lord, please deliver me
Fill my spirit this moment
With your peace, joy, and happiness
I need reassurance
Am I using the correct recipe ingredients?
If I added something that don't mix
Touch my heart so I can be obedient
Show me how to fix it
Let me never forget your recipe
The recipe of prayer for my life
I want to stay focused
On the path you set for me Lord, morning, noon, and
night
There might be times when my hurt last a while
Touch my heart each moment to moment
So through it all, I can find peace in you then smile

That Moment

I heard someone say, "If man is appointed to die than why pray for life?" We pray because we know with the Father all things are possible. In Hezekiah's situation, he was appointed to die, but his years were extended. Sometimes we may experience troubles or deeply distressed moments in our life. It feels like your heart, or soul is in so much pain. You know it is spiritual pain because you can't cure it with medicine. Right at that moment, it might seem like our prayers are not reaching the Father. We have to continue on in prayer until we get the answer, or we receive his peace.

Luke 22:41-44 (NKJV)
41 And He was withdrawn from them about a stone's throw, and He knelt down and prayed, 42 saying, "Father, if it is your will, take this cup away from Me; nevertheless not My will, but Yours, be done." 43 Then an angel appeared to Him from heaven, strengthening Him. 44 And being in agony, He prayed more earnestly. Then His sweat became like great drops of blood falling down to the ground.

Mark 14:33-36 (NKJV)
33 And He took Peter, James, and John with Him, and He began to be troubled and deeply distressed. 34 Then He said to them, "My soul is exceedingly sorrowful, even to death. Stay here and watch."

35 He went a little farther, and fell on the ground, and prayed that if it were possible, the hour might pass from

Him. ³⁶ And He said, "Abba, Father, all things are possible for You. Take this cup away from Me; nevertheless, not what I will, but what You will."

That Moment

My soul is hurting
My soul is aching Lord
Lord please heal me
Heal my natural circumstance
Heal my spiritual circumstance
My natural and spiritual pain
Is hard for me to bear alone
But with you Father all things are possible
Remove all my pain
Please touch my mind and spirit at this moment
So I won't go insane
I know prayer changes things
I ask for relief in Jesus' name
Fill my heart with love to build up my self-esteem
Stop my feelings of misery
Let me forgive
Father please forgive me
If I have done anything wrong, I truly repent
Let your Holy Spirit intercede for me
Give my soul peace and joy this moment
Let your angel of light come down and strengthen me
Oh Lord, speak a word of joy and peace in my life
If you speak it Lord, it will be done
All my spiritual and natural pain can't last
If you speak peace over me, then it will come to pass

Chapter 5 Different Scenarios & Prayers

In the second half of this book, I included some prayers on the right side of each scenario. Each prayer ends in Jesus' name, even though I didn't include it at the end of each prayer.

Lord

Lord, discipline my mind
So I can stay committed
To do what is right in your sight
Let your word have the final say so in my life
Let me measure my decision according to your words
Let me mediate on your gospels, palms, and proverbs
Let me develop the right habits
That I might tear down the enemy's strongholds
I hunger for the truth in your word dear God
Show me how to activate your power through prayer
That I might get the necessary results
Teach me how to balance a proper prayer life
As I worship you in my everyday life

What is the best way to learn how to pray? You should ask the Heavenly Father who knows all. He knows your heart and intentions. We can read every book on prayer and still be fruitless in prayer. Our prayers will be fruitless if our heart is not right, or we don't know what to ask for from the Father. One way we can be fruitful in our prayers is when the Holy Spirit makes intercession with our spirit.

Teach me how to pray

Lord, teach me how to pray
Appeal to my spiritual weakness
I ask for your goodness today
Lord, teach me how to pray
Let your Holy Spirit guide me
I crave to know your spiritual reality
I beseech you Lord
I want to learn more about you Lord
I yearn to learn your word
Lord, teach me how to pray
I long for the right words to say
I love you Lord
Let your divine love and wisdom
Fill my mind today
Let me make some time for you
So that I am able
To talk to you each day

We have to pray for each other daily. Sometimes we might have to keep our distance, but prayer knows no boundaries. The best way to communicate love towards someone is to mention them in your prayers. You should pray for their peace, joy, and well-being. You should touch, agree, and break down the strongholds together while praying for one another breakthroughs.

Our Breakthroughs are on the Way

Today is my morning
God has lifted me up
It is not the time for moaning
It is time for laughter
If I feel tired and discouraged
In prayer, I will claim my laughter
Because peace and joy
Is closer than we think
Our pains and troubles might be annoying
But they don't have to stay that way
We can tap into your source
I pray
That we pray together
Lord, please take those unpleasant things away
Replace them with peace and joy
We touch and agree in Jesus' name
Our breakthroughs are on its way
His love in our lives will reflect a positive change
Through it all, we must say
Our breakthroughs are on its way

Frequently we are blocked by our foolishness. We allow self to rule while the truth gets misconstrued. The only way we can decipher different subjects that ponder our heart is if we can get some understanding. We have to ask diligently for understanding and seek a closer relationship with the Father. Understanding is very precious because it could be the difference between life and death.

Understanding you

Heavenly Father, help me understand your kingdom
Help me understand the truth about you
Any blockage subdue
Let me exercise my free will
To get to know you
Free me from the chains
That holds me in bondage
In Jesus name
Draw me closer to you
I want to build a personal relationship with you
Help me shed sin
While I build up love
Remove any unfavorable curtains
That block out your light
Let me walk in your light
That it may consume my night
Let me walk the path
That you put in my sight
Keeping a Godly View on Life
Focused on the prize
Being led by you Jesus Christ

There are many different philosophies on how to worship. There have been many books on this subject as well. Some claim that they are the only true worshipers of God. I do believe quite a few people misunderstand the concept. True worship starts in your heart. Most people are somewhere in left field because they think worship is external. You find true worship when you tap into the true source.

Is worship

Lord, give me a mind to worship
Lord, show me how to worship
Lord, show me what worship really is
Lord, let my worship be positive
Is worship about giving?
Is worship about singing?
Is worship about hearing?
Is worship about reciting?
Is worship about dancing?
Is worship about playing?
Lord, give me a mind to worship
Let me worship
Like you want me to worship
Let me worship in servanthood
Prepare my heart for worship
Let my worship be pleasing and good
To you

The bible is just like a sign to some people. They see the no cellular phone sign posted everywhere, yet people continue to pay it no mind. Some people are blinded by their own agenda. Some people continue to use their cellular phone with no regards for the rules. There are people who attend churches today, likewise who know God's law. Some people continue to disobey it because they have their own agenda. Some people get offended when it is brought to their attention. So what good is a sign or the bible's instructions if we pay it no attention?

In fact, people can get offended by many things. The moment the pastor starts talking about similar sins that they are committing. That is why we are in desperate need of God's touch. We need that one-on-one time to discuss our life and faults with him. We need that time to ask for measurements of correction and restoration from him. It becomes easy to get blinded by self if we are not exercising our voice to have a personal conversation with the Heavenly Father.

Increase

Increase my trust in you
Increase my faith in you
Increase my love in you
Increase my knowledge of you
Increase my truth of you
Increase my understanding of you
Increase my bond with you
Increase my walk in you
Increase my talks with you
Increase my knowledge of the truth
Let me grow closer to you
Let me build up an excellent relationship with you
Guide me in prayer
Show me what to do
Increase my overall relationship with you
Each day learning something different
Walking, talking, and getting to know you

Going to church doesn't prove that you are a true Christian any more than going to school justify that you are a scholar. You must apply yourself in order to be a scholar. You must apply yourself to be a good Christian. Our instruction manual is the bible. You must not only read the bible but also apply its instructions into your everyday life. We must pray to the Lord for spiritual understanding as well. Like a new chemistry book doesn't give you knowledge not unless you study and understand the context.

I seek

My mind is open
My thoughts flow
My mind is closed, I don't know
Everything about life
I seek spiritual wisdom
I seek spiritual knowledge
I seek spiritual understanding
I seek spiritual love
I seek spiritual discretion
I seek you good Lord
I seek spiritual kindness
I seek spiritual goodness
I seek your truth
I seek your justification of me being a Christian
I seek your helping hands
Out of love
For you are love
Through you Jesus
There is nothing that I can't comprehend

I know how easy it can be to let envy creep in your heart while you are doing a service for the Lord. The enemy may send thoughts in your head like, "I wonder could they hear how great I sound." In that instance if you give in to the voice, then your service becomes a competition without you even knowing it. When those feelings arise, we have to pray on the spot. We have to ask the Lord, "Let these feelings go away. Remove the deep thoughts of competition away from me. Tune out the unprofitable voice that I may serve you in spirit and in truth."

Keeping focus in worship service

Lord I've been leading the service weekly
Once we have visitors or a program
Everyone in church is trying to outdo me
They barely lift their voice to sing
During regular worship service
They barely lift their voice to praise
During regular worship service
All of a sudden, we have musicians
That want to play now
I was the only musician
At Sunday service
They play so people can listen
And sing them praise
I perform to give you praise
This sometimes bothers me
I find myself thinking
Can anyone see or hear me
My natural thoughts kick in
I want praise from the crowd too
Deep down inside within
Lord, give me the strength to stay focused on you
Let me use my talents to uplift you
Remove the spirit of competition from my heart
I don't want to outperform everyone else
I just want to be a part
Let my talents be profitable to you
Let my thoughts stay honest and true

We live in a time where there are many versions of the truth. It is almost like the fast-food restaurant's slogan "Have it your way." You can have whatever watered down version you prefer. This still doesn't take away from the true truth. It has been truth from the beginning and will always be the truth. The truth is the word. The word is Jesus. Jesus has always been the same, but people eyes dimly see truth. The natural environment has consumed their vision. In the spiritual environment, they haven't grasped the concept yet.

In the mind of some people, they have created truth that seems right to them. They have used the bible to convince people from their point of view. Some people opinions have become truth to their followers. That is why it so important to ask our Heavenly Father to guide us in his truth. It might seem strange. If it goes against what you were taught, then it can be hard to digest. If it goes against your family, friends, current church, and or religion center of which you attend views, then there might be a conflict of interest. The truth is bigger than us and what we think. It is the truth.

Knowing Truth

Almighty God
Omnipotence, Omnipresent, and Most Holy God
Rebuild my heart
From the ground up
So I can delight in your presence
Please wake up
My sense to the truth
Reveal your spiritual reality
That I never knew
Plant my heart in divine love
Let me exercise my judgment in divine wisdom
Let your spiritual influx pass from above
Reveal your truth into my heart chamber
Help me to be a spiritual man
Not a religious man because that can present danger
Help me to understand your truth
Not my own understanding of the truth
That I learned from my youth
I seek truth
Not only to know truth
I pray that I might be able to live life accordant with
your truth
Let me talk in it
Let me walk in it
Truth

In a world, when we are surrounded by knowledge. It is easy to over flood our brains with incorrect information. There are numerous books and articles on how to get true knowledge. Many organizations claim to have the authentic version of truth. People run in search of the secret knowledge which they think is bona fide. Some of us think if it is a secret, then it must be true. The best way to obtain the true knowledge is to ask our Heavenly Father in prayer about all things pertaining to truth. He will guide us in all true knowledge.

Show me the truth

All that I have known
I know nothing
All that I have been shown
I know nothing
My education is worthless
My riches are penniless
My life achievement is mediocre
My world status is local
I seek to know knowledge
Not hidden knowledge
Base off of man self-righteousness wisdom
I seek knowledge to understand you
True knowledge begins in loving you
I seek to love you more and myself less
Self and secret knowledge brings unhappiness
Jump-start my brain with your knowledge
Undo the enemy secret embedded false knowledge
Let me look to you
When I don't understand something
Show me the truth in my personal conversation with you

Quite a lot of people get confused with going to church every time the doors open as if they are being a faithful Christian. We do need to be in the church to learn and teach others. Church begins in us. The believers within the building are our instructors. We are sometimes teachers as well. The building is just a building. Each member is part of a community, which is the church. The Holy Spirit dwells inside us. A true Christian life reflects on the outside of him or her as well as on the inside.

Truth about Church

Lord, I'm struggling with church
Some people say faith saves us
Without works
Some people say we must belong to a church
I know the church is within us
Lord, there are so many doctrines
Which one can I trust?
Lord, show me how to be a true Christian
Guide my step
Let me listen
To your Holy Spirit
Reveal the divine truth about your church
Let my life reflect your church
Let my inner spirit
Conjoin with your Holy Spirit
Guide my tongue
So, I can teach about your church
Let me be not a distraction to your church
But let me be a positive addition to your church
If I got the wrong idea about your church
Let my thoughts be rework
With accuracy about your church
Lord, I seek the truth about church

The truth has been misunderstood for years. Even in Paul's day and time, division crept into the church. We are divided over doctrine and theology. Everyone opinions and perceptions have crept into the church. Misinformed opinions and perceptions still don't make the truth false. Could we all agree that men inwardly light haven't reached its fullest potential? When the spiritual man awakens, then the truth can seep out into our lives.

There are some hard truths that we must hold firm too. There also some soft truths that we can hold yielding too. The learned and unlearned men of our time debate insignificance things. We must keep an open mind on when it comes down to debating doctrine and theology. We must pray that God guide us in all truth. We must ask our Heavenly Father, so we might not confirm things that are untrue in our heart. We must also ask our Heavenly Father to distance us from our self-understanding and self-knowledge.

We should always keep in mind that most people are at different levels of their spiritual walk. Just because they don't comprehend the truth the way you do, it doesn't mean they are not saved or a Christian. A true Christian is forever evolving into the perfect image of the Lord.

Removal of false truth

Lord, remove my perceptions
My thoughts on doctrines and theological matters
Let me add no additions
To your truth
Close my ears to substitution
Gospels and false truth
Let your truth be transparent
In my old age, youth, and adolescent
Saturate my heart with your enlightenment
Let your spiritual influx
Fill my thoughts, so I can be competent
Lord, I acknowledge I know nothing
If you give me discernment
I can uplift your truth in everything

The trinity is one of those things that will cause a debate among some people. Some people believe in it and some people don't. Depending on where you are at in your spiritual walk. Someone might be able to get you to see it their way. To the baby, in any religion, this can be mind-boggling. The best thing to do is to ask God about this matter. Take self out of the equation and let truth speak for itself.

Give me understanding

God give me understanding
On the Father, Son, and Holy Spirit
Are you one or separate?
Are there any clear distinctions?
Let me not come to my own conclusion
Let me not base my belief
Off of someone else false conclusion
I have understood it one way
Lord, I pray
If it is wrong change my heart and mind today
Resolve the matter at hand
I ask you, so I won't need any additional explanation
Clean my inner man of sin
So I can receive the right information
Let your true light shine
Into my spirit concerning this matter
Give me a receiving heart
I will remember the latter
The truth, you shall place in my spirit
Is there a trinity?
I pray to you, so I can understand
Not only let me understand
Let me be able to truthful explain it
So people can comprehend

We must be humble when delivering the truth to people. Some people won't even accept the truth if it is delivered in the wrong way. We must be conscious of people feelings. Don't be offensive while delivering the truth. Jesus taught in parables. Because he knew, certain people weren't going to be able to comprehend the truth. If you shoot straight forward, people won't listen to you. We should ask God to show us how to deliver the truth without being ugly and offensive. Some people will be more acceptable of truth if we deliver it with kindness.

How to deliver truth

Lord, bless my tongue
With a righteous breath
Let your Holy Spirit fill my lungs
So my words are gentle
Keep me humble
Your truth to me is sentimental
Let me not mumble
A bad word against my brethren
Let me speak out of love
To win over my brethren
Help me deliver the truth
In a way, they will listen
Let me be conscious when talking to the wise or youth
I know in the past, I've been shooting straight forward
My words are pushing
The people I'm trying to help backward
I want to speak the truth boldly
Let your Holy Spirit guide my lips
Let me be conscious of people's feelings while speaking
honestly

We shouldn't feel like we are walking on eggshells in our personal relationship with the Heavenly Father. We should consume the bible's knowledge and take our necessary dose of prayer consumption. By doing this, it will lead us to our comfort zone. Religion isn't supposed to be uncomfortable all the time. We will have our ups and downs. We can overcome anything along as we continue to stay in our personal relationship with God.

We have the greatest association in the universe if we line up our lives with the Father. It is a connection of love and power. Power is love, and love is power. God is love. In him, we can conquer all things through love. When we walk in the path opposite of love, we fracture our bond with God. This severs our link to the Father. If we walk in love, people can see our acquaintance with the Father. We are in union with the Holy Spirit, Father, and Son.

God I

I don't care who knows
I don't care who like me
They don't determine my destiny
Enough is enough
I resign my post at the stage of spirituality
I hang up my hat
I love you God
You have made a great impact
In my life
I will give my title back
I search not for tangible things
But a relationship with you
Which is everlasting?
Once I found you
I found the truth
I have no time anymore to rehearse
I'm falling in love with you
I'm falling in love with the spiritual church
I feel the transformation
The power of love
Lord, I give you my deepest appreciation

We must evaluate who leads us. Have we been trying to mimic someone who repeatedly goes in the wrong direction? We shouldn't follow that person to sin. What have that person gained? Is that person doing badly and spinning around in the circle? The writing is on the wall because that person's life sent up too many red flags. A red flag normally mean trouble, caution, or danger zone. We see the caution signs, so we have to realign our life to stand clear of danger. That may mean staying away from bad influences.

Stopping the cycle

Lord, I am following
Help me be a leader
I see the way they are living
But Lord I'm still following
I don't know why?
I try to stop
But I am trapped by me
I see their reality
I see they are not making any positive progression
I see their many scams for money
I see their regression
Lord, I'm mimicking the wrong person
I chose a worldly mentor for a lesson
Lord, restore me to you
So I can receive my blessings
My family has told me the truth
I thought they didn't understand because of my youth
Lord, help me
I'm spinning around in a circle
That is insanity
Lord, make me sane
Today help me change

Your purpose begins with you asking the Lord to prepare you for the mission that he has set for your life. You must be willing to accept it in love while taking on his characteristics and embracing his love. Our unity with God should be in love because it helps us to stay in fellowship with him. It will help us subdue any obstacles in life. Once we grow closer to our Heavenly Father, we better understand God's love. When we possess this type of love, then we can be better ministers of his word.

A word of love

I want to take on your characteristics
Inspect me through and through
That I might know my own logic
I want to bring productivity
So I can deliver character
As I minister for your glory
I don't want to make it complex
Let me simplify the message
But still teach the truth
With plenty of love and less aggression
So when the word is taught
The hearer of the word learns a lesson
That is valuable to the ear
A word that makes them fall in love
Because the power of God is near
A word of love
That pricks their hearts for you dear God

If I ask the question, do you have an idol? Most people will automatically think of a created thing that people worship. An idol can be something that we don't think of as being an idol. Matter of fact, some people has idols, and they don't even know it. It may be hidden. God will have to reveal it to you before you see it. It doesn't have to be a bad habit. It can be something so special and honest, however, you direct all your time toward it. An idol is anything that hinders us from serving God. We should pray and ask God to show us our hidden idol if we have one.

Removing hidden idols

I thought idols could only be
Sculptors or graven images
I never knew it could be
Something so innocent
Something so pure in reality
I pray for balance over my life
I pray to do well
In your sight
Lord, reveal any hidden idols
That I can't see
If I love anything more than you
Please show me
Uplift me
Renew me
Remove that idol
Far from me
I pray that you balance my time
I pray to keep you first in my mind

After our self-evaluation, we must pray for our wife, husband, children, etc..... that they might receive a wakeup call and realize their faults. Over and over again, we pray for natural results. It is common to pray for their external wellbeing. We must pray that God work on them from the inside out, so he can wash their spiritual man. Once the spiritual results are achieved, then the natural results will line up.

Bless my spouse

Lord, lift up your hands over my spouse
When my spouse is struggling
Show my spouse the way out
I see my faults
You have revealed them to me
Lord, reveal my spouse faults
So my spouse might see
The errors of my spouse wicked ways
Give my spouse divine love
Bless my spouse each and every day
I pray
Fill my spouse's spirit with your Holy Spirit
So my spouse can change
I pray for a spiritual change
As well as a natural change
In Jesus name
Heal our house
Cleanse my spouse

So many people imagined a different future for their lives when they were younger. I saw a difference future for myself as well. Even, I had to come to the understanding that my plan might not be God's plan. Does that make it easy to accept? Sometime, No! It is a great thing that God knows us. If we had the power, some of our lives would be rotten to the core. Our spiritual life will be neglected. God has a plan for us and majority of the time his plan is not our plan. We have to tap back into the source. We have to ask God what his plan for our life is.

.

Tapping back into the source

God, I tap back into your source
You have brought me this far
I do rejoice
Sometimes I don't understand
Why this, why that
Lord, you hold my hand
You know the hearts of man
You know what we think
How we comprehend
I thought, "I would be a rich man"
I thought, "I would own acres of land"
You know my heart
For me, you had a different plan
I surrender to your plan
For my life
If I line up with you
My dream will take flight
Take the fog away
So I can see your plan for my life
As clear as day
Let my actions line up
As your plan crush
Anything that tries to hinder it
Let me walk in my purpose
Let me move in it

We set up defense mechanisms that will protect our feelings. It is put in place for the right reasons to protect self. It becomes problematic when it starts overriding our reality with false truth. It will be tough for someone to give us decent advice. It will be even harder for us to accept it. When our defense mechanisms take control, we only see what we see. This sometimes is the only right we know from experiences.

The line is drawn in the sand. You can no longer see black and white. You see distance darkness. Your thoughts are in overdrive to protect self. The light is far from you. With God's power, we can override our thoughts and emotions. We can reformat our hard drive to boot up in a positive direction. By spending time in God's presence, we can learn this. We can learn how to transform our thoughts and reactions to agree with him.

Defense mechanisms

Lord, let me listen to decent advice
Let me have the heart of acceptance
If it is right
Keep my emotions in check
Let me respond with no disrespect
My defense mechanisms are for my protection
Lord, I thank you for it
Separate me from confusion
I'm trusting in you
My strength lies in you
Conduct my direction
Therefore, I lack nothing
All of my life provisions
Are from you
I willingly accept
Your blessings are nutriment for my soul
Sustain my cup and correct my footsteps
Keep my defensive mechanisms in line with your precepts

As soon as, we set up self-defense mechanisms for religion our mind is blocked. It is hard for us to listen to someone else's perspective. We will immediately shut them down. This raises our level of intake of acceptance for any other religion.

It shuts us down from effectively communicating with other people. This can be disturbing to our spiritual health. Our inhospitable conduct can cause us to miss out on some useful information. We must remain mild while protecting the truth. We must stay open to intake new thoughts, as long as it lines up with the truth. Bitter religion defense mechanisms soar discord.

Religion defense mechanisms

Take off my religious clothing
Unloose my ego
Take away my titles
My self-righteousness
And self-promotion
My external religion serves no purpose
Let my religion be internal
On life center stage
Search my heart
In my heart, I want to be a member
A member of your church
Where I can be mature
Where the environment is nourishing
Where great value is placed on love
Where we impress only you
Where our hearts are made to serve
Where I can grow
Daily in your word
Where I can learn how to react
Walking the straight walk
With a positive impact
Under the guidance of your wisdom
I reject any negative religion defense mechanisms

Some prayer warriors who spend time in the presence of the Father could easily forget about praying for themselves. They could spend so much time interceding for everyone else that other people problems become the center of their attention. Almost like a mechanic who has a broken-down car, but he will fix everyone else's car but his own. Interceding is a great duty and great gift from God. Yet instill prayer warriors must not forget to pray for themselves. For some prayer warriors, this might seem selfish. They live to pray for others.

You must not forget to ask our Father about yourself. Prayer is the key to the soul and the light of our life, as well as a great tool to intercede for others. When we visit our Father in prayer, we can do our spiritual checkup with the greatest physician ever.

A blessing for me

Thank you Heavenly Father
Thank you Heavenly Father
I know you hear my prayers
I pray to you daily
Because I enjoy talking to thee
I don't want to sound selfish
I thank you for loving me
I don't want to sound self-righteous
I stand in your presence
In the need of prayer
Your humble servant
Heavenly Father
I ask for blessings for my family
Please Lord, don't forget to bless me
Let me be engulfed in your
Love, peace, happiness, and tranquility
Let me live life pleasing to thee
Uncover my shortcomings
Please remove them from me
So you can, continue to bless me
As I continue to praise thee

A lot of times we think that we are not the problem. A true Christian must do a self-evaluation on himself or herself. We must ask the Lord to reveal our surface and hidden problem areas in our life. When our hidden problem areas are revealed, it can help us escape bondage. This is the only way we can live lives of transparency in Christ when we ask God to help us perform a self-evaluation on ourselves.

Reveal myself to myself

Lord, reveal myself to myself
Unfold the inner me
What is my inner truth?
I pray for transparency
Let me look into the mirror
Transform my thoughts
So my self-evaluation is clearer
Let me be aware of my wrong
Let me correct it that very moment
So, that my sin won't linger on
Free me from self-bondage
I loose old baggage
I loose hidden luggage
That is standing in my way
Lord, fix my life today
Better my situation
Let me not blame others
For my limitations
Help me grow stronger in you
When I perform my self-evaluation

When we try to conquer sin, it won't lie down and just let us be. It will put up a fight. Once you try to escape its holds, get ready for the battle. We must continue to pray for the thoughts that hold us in prison.

Example:
Lord, "Help me stop thinking about lusting after her." Then the very same moment a thought appears, ("You know you want her, so stop praying for that").

When that thought occurs, that can put you in an unusual position. In that very moment, you must ask God to help you with that sin. Ask him to remove that inner lust from your heart, so you can continue serving him.

Fighting Sin

Prepare me for battle
The war is already waged
Sin has taken center stage
I tried to escape its hold
I'm losing control
The more I tried to escape
I'm being led back in
I fought once before
Sin aims its arch at me again
I fought once more
It targeted me through my friends
When I open my door
I prayed today
I fell anyway
Lord, I call on you
This moment, please renew
My strength in you
Place your armor around me
Don't let me give up or retreat
Let me fight it with your help
Until my sins meet its defeat

There are people who have no ambitions that have been cast out by society. They find comfort in solitude. Everyone has cast them aside. Those people think that there is no hope for the future, but there is hope of a brilliant future. We all can have a bright future because embedded in us all is the sense to belong to our creator. We can release all regrets and neediness. We can find ourselves while communicating with our Father. He will console us in the hardest times in our lives. God will be our source of good intentions. We can find him in prayer at any time.

Sharer of blessings

Build up my self-esteem
Take away my low expectations
Delay my quick gratifications
Retrain my thought process
Poor thinking won't change my situation
Infuse my power supply
Remove my animal nature
Give me a servant mentality
Refuel my quality of life
Increase your participation
Give me the strength to walk upright
Let me change the culture
In you, I can set flight
Align my thoughts on your system
Align my actions to walk in wisdom
Change my nature, values, principles, and patterns
Release your blessings
So I can be a sharer of blessings

Many people use material things to hide behind. They have several uncertainties in life. They think cars, riches, and clothes etc.... determine their self-worth. True self-worth is to have an ongoing relationship with our Heavenly Father. Once you know God then you know those other things really don't matter. They were only a placeholder and not a good placeholder at that. You know that placeholder which serves no purpose but only to hold up time or space.

True self-worth

Open my eyes to see my self-worth
I can't get it from a new car
A new pair shoes or a name brand shirt
I can only receive it from you
You hold everything true
I know my self-worth
I don't have to sleep around
I don't have to impress anyone in church
I know my self-worth
I don't have to go to the latest concert
I don't have to follow the latest trend
I'm very important
I'm not trying to fit in
I don't need the President's approval
To some I might be unusual
I know myself
I'm slowly dying to self
As I look in the mirror
Lord, continue to direct my steps
Continue to change me
Into the Christian, you want me to be
As I advance in your glory

Often, we try to take preventive steps to protect our heart. We try to prepare for each situation, as if we can change the outcome. We can't alter the situation if we don't spend time in prayer. Prayer will help us release our worries and stress. Through prayer we can give it to God and be worriless.

It is awesome that we can petition the creator of the universe for anything our heart desires. Oh how blessed, we are in this day in time. There was a time when a certain nation (Israel) had the only right to petition God as his chosen people. Nevertheless now, we can ask our Heavenly Father on a personal level to help us with preventive measurements.

Release my worry & stress

I tried my best to settle the matter at hand
Every time, I perceived victory; things got out of hand
I can't understand your wisdom
I can't comprehend
Your righteousness and blessings
Right now, I give my problems to you, Lord
I'm confessing
I can't alter or fix my situation
I can't worry or stress my problems away
I'm faced with many obligations
I have no solution
But my problems are many
Filling my spirit like pollution
Today I claim triumph in the storm
I conquer everything that is not of you
I stand in your favor
My heart is glad because I am getting to know you
Lord, protect my heart
Breathe your breath in me
So I can begin a new start
Let my life be
Carefree and worry-free

In prayer, you find a clear vision of purpose. You must ask the right questions. Success is all about asking the right questions. The right questions are not the same for you or me. It is whatever weight that is weighing down in your heart that causes you to be unsuccessful. What does your soul crave to know? Your soul craves the keys to your success of your inner spirit. What God has set up for you is true success. Knowing your purpose through prayer and walking in it is the greatest success one can achieve. It is discovered in your personal relationship with the Heavenly Father.

Reconnecting

I'm anxious Lord
I need to stay connected to the source
It is evitable Lord
You are my number one choice
I can't alienate you
It is obvious
I can only change in you
Not just a simple change
But a life renewal change
A drastic change
Because only you can make me whole
I want to have long lasting conversations with you
That is reconnecting for my soul
Enter my heart chamber
Speak to my soul
I want to be your child not a stranger
Let me respond to your call
I want to be on one accord with you
Pick me up when I fall
Put on my heart the right questions
Let me show gratitude for every blessing
When you speak
Let me listen and enjoy the message

This might be a time of confusion in your life. You are hitting the crossroad of your spiritual journey and natural life. You are beneath the butt of disappointment after disappointment. You might be in the middle of a spiritual growth spurt. Now is not the time to give up but keep persevering. Look to God, which is where your help comes from, and seek God out in his word and through prayer.

There you will find the answers for your questions. There you will find peace for your soul. There you will find comfort and a warm place from the cold.

I call on you

My thoughts are so confused
It is like jumbled up soup
I feel tired and used
As I walk, bend, and stoop
I don't know what to ask for
What really makes sense?
I'm under false pretense
I've been misused by the pastors
I've been overlooked by the prophets
I've been taught wrongly by the teachers
I can't catch a break
The minister lashed out at me when I made a mistake
No one cares for me
So it may seem Lord
I call on you Lord
Deliver me
Mend my conscience
Revitalize the way I think
Revamp your truth all through me

Sometimes we think back over our life and think what if. It is almost like our past is a blur in time. We replay it trying to make sense of our current situation. If we have any doubts about the choices, which we have made in the past, then we can ask God for clarity on how our past led us to this moment. Let us not get too caught up in the past. The past is the past for a reason. We only have this moment and the next moment also if God allows us to live. We should consider every moment as an opportunity to build a great relationship with him.

Asking for Clarity

Today I look back over my life
Lord, what have I done thus far to get to this point
Whether wrong or right
I search for simplicity
I search for clarity
Right now everything looks blurry
I pray that you help me see things clearly
Today I won't ponder over my past
What if, what if this, what if that
I will not holdfast
But this present moment
I will uplift your name
My life isn't an accident
Despite my circumstances
You have blessed me and given to me
This very moment another chance

We should always pray for clarity on what God wants us to do. If we are not spiritual prepared, it may be easy to be deceived. The enemy will always try to interrupt our walk with God. We can get confused if we are not tuned into the right channel. We must have an open line of communication with our Father so that beyond a shadow of doubt we will know his voice. We should pray that we only hear God's voice. We should pray that God block out the enemy's voice.

Open my ears to you

Tune my ears to the right channel
I seek your approval
Give me discernment to hear your voice
Let me not be led by a counterfeit voice
I seek your wisdom
In my every choice
I don't want to be misled
I feel my gut and inner voice
Keep my emotions in check
So, I won't get distracted by any noise
If it isn't you Lord
I don't want to hear
If it is, you Lord.
Open my ears
So I can receive it crystal clear
Help me tune in with clarity
That I might keep your love near
Is my gut feeling, correct?
Regardless of what I feel
Let your truth manifest

A bad relationship can paralysis your spiritual growth. While you try to elevate to higher levels, your associate might try to keep you on a downward spiral to the bottom. We have to stay true to God. A bad associate will make normal praying inevitable for you to grasp. The moment you are in your prayer closet or kneeling to pray then they will come in and rudely interrupt you. A bad associate feels as though you wasted your time because they can't see your results yet. Their eyes are closed to the impossible because they haven't discovered the value of prayer.

You know it works, so you have to stay on course. A bad associate can only see their countless disappointments about life. You can't let their negativity affect your thoughts. You have to let God impact your negative thoughts with positive reinforcements. Always pray for that person's negative perspective to change to a positive perspective. You must pray for their breakthrough. In your prayer time, ask our Father for a silent place, so you can enjoy his presence along with his peace and stillness.

Peace in my secret place

Lord, let me find you in my secret place
Even though somebody is causing a distraction
Cover me with your warm embrace
I pray for my surroundings
I ask for a blessing
They can't see what I see
As I begin to speak
They rudely disturb me
Bless their countless disappointments
Remove their resentments
Change their hearts
Let them follow closer to you dear God
Break through their hurt and pain
I know they wonder why I still pray
I'm not ashamed
I found power, peace, joy, and love
In Jesus name
You make my inevitable
Evitable
When I pray, things change
I pray for their positive perspective
In the mighty Jesus name

As employees, we are obligated to do an honest day's work on the job. We are working for God and not for man. They are just in a position of authority. I know sometimes it seems like the whole world is on our shoulders. It seems like we can't win because our work may go unnoticed. The more effort we put into our tasks could cause less desirable results.

It may seem like the only people who get recognized on the job are the people who aren't performing to standard. We must understand that we work for God and not man. We can't underwork ourselves as a Christian employee because, whatever, we do reflect on our Lord. We don't have to overwork ourselves either. We should ask the Lord to help us in this area with the perfect balance over our work life.

An Honest Day's Work

They are playing buddy-buddy games
I can't get ahead
Every company seem like the same
No boss stands for truth
It seems that every HR department
Is trying to pursue
Nothing but unrighteousness
I'm trying to stand firm
In the mix of this wickedness
I don't want to work hard
Because my deeds are unnoticed
I try to keep you in my heart
My work ethics is falling apart
Lord place in my soul the truth
I know I'm not working for them
I'm working for you
Give me balance
So I won't underwork myself
Give me the balance
So I won't overwork myself
But give me balance
So I will give my employer an honest day of work

As a leader in our place of employment, God has blessed us with these jobs. We have an obligation to lead, as God wants us to lead. We have to take care of his people. We are in charge for one reason because God has allowed us to be good steward over his children. We will be held accountable for our actions as leaders. Even if we escape this life unharmed, there is a bigger price to pay. We could lose our soul for not being fair. We should pray for guidance on how to lead other people the way God wants us to lead them.

Help me lead

Lord, help me become a great leader
Train my thoughts
Let me follow truth and fairness at all costs
Correct my words before they leave my lips
Help me build up positive relationships
Help me lead your people
Help me to be slow to wrath
But quick to treat everyone as equal
Let me be no push over
Protect me and my team
Carry us on your shoulder
Let me not be afraid to speak
Let me speak first with love
Let me be bold but not weak
Let your light shine through me
Bless my surroundings
With peace and tranquility
Let me be the leader that you want me to be

Sometimes we run into trials and tribulations. We might feel like our lifeline is gone. Some people grasp for their last breath. At that very moment, it is so easy to forget about, who we are in the Lord. They may begin to doubt when that happen their faith fails. We must keep on praying and praising the Lord. Also we must keep on walking in faith because our Heavenly Father is working it out. We should never give in to doubt but cling to our victory. Through prayer, we should claim our assured victorious results.

Heavenly Father you are

Heavenly Father, show me which way to go
My head is hanging low
My strength is weak
I've been experiencing restless nights with no sleep
I've been having an extra crazy week
I've been experiencing problems after problems
I extend my heart to you in prayer
Lord, you can solve them
You are my King of King
Through you I'm redeemed
My health lies in your hands
My life has been changed
Through you I live and understand
You are my problem solver
As I speak right now
My life is shaping up because of your love for me Father
I believe in positive change
I know change is on the way
Lord you are my lifeline
It shall happen this moment, minute, or day

As soon as you begin to make your transformation in God, majority of the time, you will not have the home team cheering you on. The home team will be cheering for the visiting team. Oh yes, they will cheer against you. Because some people won't understand that by you accepting God in your life how your life will change for the better. They may not understand how God is moving in your life now. They might think that they are helping you out by making interventions. They might even question why you don't do certain things anymore like going to the club, smoking weed and cigarettes, or drinking.

This makes the journey to transformation difficult to endure. You might even want to quit. Please don't quit. This is the time to continue on your journey of new discovery because you are on the road to recovery. You must continue to pray and seek God in prayer. At the same time, God will gradually heal your spirit in the mist of your transformation.

Transformation

Every time I get into a disagreement
Somebody yell, "I thought you was a Christian"
I'm trying to realign my life for my betterment
The world expects me to be perfect
Even though my bad actions
I regret
I'm struggling with my transformation
I'm catching pressure direct and indirect
From my coworkers, friends, and family
Now my motive is suspect
To the world
My transformation is a counterfeit
Lord, keep the passion in me
So, I won't quit
I need this transformation
I know you are cheering me on
I pray that your Holy Spirit
Touch my thoughts as I move along
Transforming in your image of love
Shedding off the spirit of anger and fear until they are
gone

Habitually we try to prepare for different situations ourselves. We have different scenarios planned out of what we think should be the best solutions. It might seem reasonable and sensible at the time. We mess up when we take God out of the decision-making process. We should always ask God to prepare us for the best decision according to his will. We should be eager to ask like King David asked God before he went into battle.

Keeping you in my decision process

Lord, I am tired of leaving you out of my decision process
Every action
I try to perform on my own end up in failure
I ask on my behalf
Because I only know half
You know the whole situation
I know you are working it out
But I need help with my patience
Your timing isn't mine
My solution might not be in line
With your perfect will
Yet instill
I try to run my life race fast
When your spirit is telling me to stand still
It will come to pass
Because it is not my war
I ask for your guidance
So, I won't fall into life's lure

We spend several hours of the day petitioning the Father for health, money, cars, food, and clothing. We seek him for material things. The majority of us very seldom pray to know more about his divine love. Love is what holds the universe together. God is love. While praying for everything else under the sun, we should also pray for divine love.

Divine Love

Lord, I don't seek the usually
I pray for divine love
Fill my heart today
With your divine love
Sit on your throne
In my heart with your presence
With you, I'm not alone
Fill my surroundings with your divine love
I seek no material blessings
I petition you Father of love
I ask for spiritual blessings
In your son name
In divine love
Let divine love fill every crack of my life
Let divine love correct my wrong
So they may be right
Let no hatred have no part
In my life
Let divine love fill my heart
This day, this night

I have watched several people who don't know, when to hold on or when to let go. People get confused with patience by settling for less. You don't want to throw in the towel at first sight. You shouldn't want to hold on to just anything either. You have to find that common ground. There is a difference in being complacent and being patient.

Not settling for less

Lord, you have the final say
I've been feeling a longing for you
Show me the way
I seek to learn the difference between contentment
And being complacent
I'm content; you breathe life in my life
I'm not complaining Lord
I'm very grateful
I don't want to settle Lord
In you I can accomplish all things
Help me accomplish them with wisdom
True knowledge that wisdom brings
Show me the difference between patience
Or just settling and waiting
When I need to press forward
Give me joy and peace
As I press toward
My purpose you have set for me
Keep your hand over my life
Let me feel your tranquility

Sometimes we ask for patience while thinking patience will magically appear without going through something. In the mist of some people patience walk, they want to abandon it. At that moment, they will ask God to fix the problem right then in there. Somehow their prayers for patience are far from their lips. In order to gain patience, we must go through tribulations. We must not abandon patience. We should ask God for some wisdom to understand patience. We should believe that God would give us strength and momentum to endure our situations to the end with patience if he doesn't fix it right away.

Obtaining patience

My life is a disaster Lord
My burdens are too heavy right now for me to bear
I'm going through something at home and at work
Lord, I need your spiritual warfare
Every time I look up something is about to explode
The enemy has just reloaded
Another heartache which caused me to be upset because
of the pain
The pressure of life still remains
Sometimes I feel like it is hard to maintain
Life has a way of eating away at you
I remember that I asked for patience
I never knew
In order to receive patience
I will have to endure some uncomfortable situations
Lord, help me obtain this precious attribute
Shine your light and water my spiritual root
In my suffering and pain help me keep your statutes
While I bring forth fruits

Our Heavenly Father is the greatest physician I know. We are blessed to be able to call on him in our time of need. When our primary care doctor is off duty, our great physician is always on duty. God is in the healing business. God can heal your inner man as well as your outer man. Our Heavenly Father wants us to be complete. The only way we can be complete is to have good health. We should always pray for other people good health as well as our own good health in our prayers.

Bless my health

I am feeling fatigue
I pray for strength
Lord be my strength
Replace this feeling of sickness
With the feeling of healthiness
Replenish my health
For health is one of your blessings
I know that I can't do it myself
So to you Lord, I'm confessing
Restore my spiritual body
Restore my natural body
Exchange this feeling of queasiness
Heal my condition
Cure my infection
Destroy my disease
Kill the virus inside of me
Let me feel relief
Exchange my nausea and vomiting
For your heavenly delight
Restore me whole to good health again
Restore my weak body and spirit with your strength
Shower me with your blessings of perfect health over and
over again

In life we can let our problem defeat us, or we can defeat our problems through speaking positive thoughts over our life and current situations. The moment you begin, things start to shift in a more achieving way. When we step into favor and being optimistic, the whole world is our oasis. Positive thoughts foster your environment.

Some might say how can you stay positive?

Once you understand true love and tap into the source being positive is just a state of mind. It comes with the new uniform. So every morning when you suit up, put on the armor of God. Don't forget your positive attitude.

Positive thoughts

I pray for my breakthrough
Anxieties has no place near me
I place health problems, money troubles
Along with any issues affecting my family
In the palm of your hand
Lord, you can handle it
Much better than I can
I pray for my breakthrough
Before I knew you
I felt like, I couldn't get through
You are a provider
As I pray now to you
I see clearer
I'm satisfied
I pray for my breakthrough
My mind is being renewed
My favor is being restored
My love is being overflowed
I see my breakthrough
My yokes are all destroyed
I pray Lord, I speak in Jesus' name
Nothing can hold me back
Everything that was a hinder doesn't remain
I'm growing in love, power, and servanthood
I pray Lord, help me abstain
I see my breakthrough
With you there is nothing hard to obtain

We don't have to always ask for something while we are praying. Sometimes we should reflect on God's goodness. We can give him the glory and just reflect on our life with praise and thanksgiving. We can talk and share our emotions with our Heavenly Father. Through our daily praying, we can embrace his kindness and be thankful. We can just thank our Heavenly Father out of the blue because he has just brought us through a situation. We can just praise him because we feel his presence. You never need a reason to praise, pray, and give thanks to God.

Sharing emotions of praise

Glorious Father
Thank you for the gift
The gift of life
Thank you for creating me
With your limitless thoughts of creation
I thank you because you thought of me
Every day you breathe the breath of life in my lungs
Your Holy Spirit helps me to overcome
Your divine love is the same everyday
I thank you Heavenly Father
Sometimes sin block my way
But Hallelujah and praise to you Father
Separated from you
I don't have to stay
Once I repent and get back focused on you
Your throne is open to me when I pray
Hallelujah, Hallelujah
Thank you Heavenly Father this day

How can we let go of madness when someone continues to offend us? It seems as if the bible is outdated when it comes to this. Your natural reaction is to retaliate or remove that person from your life completely. It seems like a no-win situation. We must pray that God would hold our tongue and heart. We must pray that God will help us stay in Christian Character.

Replace madness with love

Lord, I have extended my hand
Of forgiveness once again
This person is annoying
I feel like he (she) is playing off of me being a Christian
I grow ire
In his (her) presence
I want to attack with hostility
I want to engage with rage
I forgave him (her) several times before
My madness is taking center stage
My anger has reached its limit
I'm fed up with it
All his (her) insults

I'm about to step out of my Christian Character
Lord, fix my situation
Take away any thoughts of retaliation
Help me disregard those smart remarks
Let me answer him (her) with kindness
God jump-start my heart
Give me the strength to truly forgive him (her)
Help me extend some grace
Let me show divine love toward him (her)
So I can win him (her) into the faith

(I drew a line to separate the 2nd part of this prayer. You can repeat the second part any time you feel like retaliating or removing someone from your life. There is no need to repeat the 1st half after you have spoken to God about it. The reason being is because you want to remain positive as you can while defeating the enemy)

When we have just been offended, it is hard to keep
our emotions in check sometimes. We are human
beings. We are emotional. The thoughts of love are far
from our mind once offense is present. The thoughts of
revenge somehow draw nearer in the present of
offense. In that split second, when those feelings arise,
we must pray to God to remove those feelings. If we are
not careful, those feelings could become permanent
hidden feelings toward a person. Majority of the times,
those feelings start out small but eventually build up
into humongous mountains over time.

Remove those feelings

Be my protector Lord
Guide my emotions right now
I can taste that bitter revenge Lord
Even though I know your love is sweet
Let your divine love console me
Take away that bitter taste off of my tongue
For my victory is already won
I will trade my thoughts of revenge for grace
I bless right now instead of curse
I love right now instead of hate
You have shown me my fate
Wash away my bitterness
For only your love is pure sweetness
So fill my heart with your love right now Lord
Because the enemy is trying to provoke me
My Lord
Revenge is not for me
In spite of my circumstances
Allow me to love constantly

It seems every time we start trying to line our life up with God, there is a person or situation in our life that tries to hinder the process. The enemy knows how to get us to the point that our water boils over. It happens right after we say, "I'm not going to let that person or situation get me angry anymore." We must pray to God when anger tries to settle over us. God is our number one defense system against anger. We can override anger with God's love every time.

Replacing anger with tranquility

Let anger have no place in me
Let anger lose its battle to calmness
Let me find comfort in serenity
When my anger
Engage my temper
Because of the firer within me present a current danger
Let me sit still and find quietness
Let me bathe in your inner peace
Let me redirect my rage in the stillness
Lord, give me composure when I'm agitated
Take away any negative impulses or reactions in the
moment of my weakness
Lord like me proceed with caution
In my wrath or fury
Let me find comfort in you
Let me find tranquility
For there is no place in my heart for anger or rage
Lord, fill my life center stage
With calmness, peace, and divine love

Once we are offended by one person. It is so easy to have ill feeling toward their whole family. When we enter their family's presence, we might feel uncomfortable and sometimes frustrated for no reason at all. Our anger could play off of the first situation while carrying it over to the next situation. A lot of times, we are still mad at the original person, so we assume that their family has something against us as well. It is much easier to believe this, because of the old saying, "blood is thicker than water." There could be some tension but nine time out of ten it is all in our head. We can only escape this trap through prayer.

A healing of peace

My frustration has kicked in gear
I feel anger
Every time they are near
They did nothing to me
My reaction every time
Is not what it should be
When anger guide my thoughts
I feel like they are out to get me
They haven't done anything wrong
I'm confused because my anger for my offender
Is so strong
I blame their whole family

⟵————————————————⟶

Lord, take away my hurt and my awkward feeling
Take away my need to blame everyone else
Let love fill my heart so I can start my healing
Heal my emotions
Remove my negative thoughts
Let me feel nothing but goodness
Toward my offender and their family
Cover me with your peace

(I drew a line to separate the 2nd part of this prayer. You can repeat the second part any time you feel the feeling of anger or blaming coming on. There is no need to repeat the 1st half after you have spoken to God about it. The reason being is because it will reopen old wounds.)

Once we feel like someone has wronged us, it is hard to make amends. Sometimes we say we have forgiven that person or persons but deep down inside, we hold on to hurt and distrust. A red flag is if we can't stand to see that person in our presence. A feeling of bitterness may fill the atmosphere. How can we conquer this feeling and really forgive from the inner man? We must pray for this healing of our heart. We must pray also for our broken relationships to be healed. Our Heavenly Father is able to fill our bitterness with sweetness. Oh how sweet it is like good old honeydew. Our Heavenly Father will touch our old bitter hearts and make them new.

True forgiveness

Bitterness, anger, and mistrust
My heart ache with disappointment
I gave them my trust
Out of my lips come the words I forgive
But in my heart
Frustration still lives
How long will my madness last
I say, "I put it in my past"
It keeps on reappearing
Like salt on an open wound
Bitterness is still steering
My life
Inside hatred is stealing
My peace, joy, and love

Lord, I need a healing
Replace everything on my inside with divine love
Change my atmosphere
So I can stay clear
Of hatred, envy, and strife
So true forgiveness
Can fortify my life

(I drew a line to separate the 2nd part of this prayer. You can repeat the second part any time you feel madness coming on. There is no need to repeat the 1st half after you have spoken to God about it. The reason being is because you don't want your negative thoughts to override your positive thoughts.)

It is a common thing for most people to think that they are always right. We can get into a habit of praying our enemies out of our life. We might pray that they be removed from our church, our home, and our workplace etc.... At the same time, they might be praying to God about you. We shouldn't get to absorb in self-righteousness always thinking that we are always right. Majority of the time, that isn't the case. We have to be careful when praying people out of our life. We must make sure that we aren't the one who is standing in the need of fixing. It can be a very awkward moment if we are praying for someone else removal, but God reveals to us that we are the one who needs fixing.

Blessing My Enemies

Lord, I know my foe and I claim self-righteousness
because we attend church
Or we seem to be religious because we read the bible and
pray
We continually pray that our enemies be removed from
church or work
Or even out of our life
Because in our minds, we are the one who is right
Lord, I know you hear our prayers
My opponent and I curse each other continually sending
up prayers
Neither one of us is aware

Of our faults
We continue to ask for each other removal
Our prayers ascending like saltless salt
But today, Lord, I don't pray for their removal
I pray that we both see our faults
I pray that we might be filled with the fruit of the spirit
I pray that we might walk in the spirit
I pray for positive change
Lord, let your blessings rain
Let no negativity remain
If they are unwilling to accept positive change
In this current environment
Change their environment
So they can accept positive change
Let me accept positive change
Wherever my opponent may go
Lord, let your blessings continually flow
Today I learned my lesson
I pray for our blessings

Some people tend to get influenced by a whole lot of things. That is why it is always good to ask God to change our intake, so that it is favorable to his will. We don't want to have to count or guard ourselves against everything like counting calories. Counting calories manually can be time-consuming. We want to automatically pick up on those things that damage our spirit. We can ask God to help us in this area. With God's help, we will overcome sin every time it enters our presence.

Change my intake

Place in my mind newness
Lord, change my intake
What I read
What I watch on television
What I say in my conversations
What I listen to on my radio
That I might have spiritual freedom
Let me not conform to old patterns
Let me start new patterns
So I can reflect an attitude of spiritual maturity
Let me have the right thoughts
Let me have the right actions
Let me keep my motivation
Let me find heaven on earth
Let me find the power of serving you Lord
Let me not seek after gratitude
Let me seek after pure worship of you Lord
Activate my spiritual life
So my natural offering is prompted by your love
To operate in you Lord as the head of my life
In Mighty name of Jesus Christ

It seems like when we participate in religion, there are lots of dos or don'ts. Religion has been stretched from the simpler version into a more complex version. Religion can be so complex that not even some of our modern-day bible scholars truly understand it. So many people are caught up with a false illusion that they put on a show for the church every Sunday. They try to perform for God. God needs no stellar performance. All God expect is for us to worship and praise him from our heart in spirit and truth.

Simpler version

I don't want to get involved in the
Laundry list of things to do
Or the school rules of things
I shouldn't do
When I'm participating in religion
I don't want to be loaded down
Or feel pressure to perform
Just for external reasons
I can never gain your approval God on my own
Let me focus on my internal spirit
Not behavior modifications
That draws my fear for external consequences
Fill me with your Holy Spirit
With vigor, good health, and everlasting love
Pour your Holy Spirit into my lungs
Take away my sin nature
My desire to please myself
That I might take the center stage of life
I don't want a stellar performance
Let my reality mimic the ways of love shown by your son
Jesus Christ
I am striving for the simpler version
Religion of the heart
Not the complex version
Putting on a show for the people just to be a part
Of the in-crowd
I just want to worship and praise you
And live a blessed and loving lifestyle

Some people get so frustrated that they stop communicating with God. We have to stay focused on God. God isn't like our associate who we can turn our back on and walk away from. How can you walk away from someone one who is omnipresence? It is simple because you can't. You must never get to discourage over your destructive decisions that it causes you to stop chatting with our Heavenly Father because this will only make the problems get worst. We have to ask God for help continuously, so we can deal with the consequences. We must be reassured by the fact that God will never leave us or never disown us.

Back closer to you

Lord, pull me out
I am insecure or unsure
Where I stand in my relationship with you
I had a relationship with you
Once I called on you
All the time
I unintentionally drifted away
I lost our relationship over time
I lost my breathtaking experiences
When I got lost in my accomplishments
Father, I need your awe-inspiring presence
It was splendid
I want to get back closer to you
Change how I impact other people
My success is not a substitute
Change what I feel, my choices, and the way I think
Let my love for you shine through
Immerse me in your Holy Spirit
So I can just enjoy you
Let me enjoy our long conversations
I stand in the need of
An internal spiritual transformation

Quit suppressing yourself by depressing yourself. Speak life into your life. It is what it is. It is what it could be. You have the next moment, minute, or day if God allows you to stay on his beautiful earth. You must know that you don't have to be anything that is the opposite of love. Speak life in your life to receive life. You must know God is life and through him, we receive life. For the scriptures say, "I can do all things through Christ Jesus who strengthen me." If you believe that you have freedom through Christ Jesus, then you have freedom through Christ Jesus. Your freedom starts with a thought, so turn your negative thoughts toward your newfound freedom in Christ Jesus.

I speak life in my life

I can have total freedom in every area of my life
I don't have to be limited by finances
I don't have to be stressed out
I don't have to be frustrated
I don't have to be full of anxiety
I don't have to be fearful
I don't have to be complacent
I don't have to live constrained
I don't have to live in spiritual darkness
I can walk in light
I can find freedom
In your full salvation
I have freedom in my success
I have freedom in my finances
I have freedom in my health
I have freedom in my family
I have freedom through Christ
To live the abundant life
I will not suppress myself
I will not depress myself
I speak life in my life
Through the blood of Jesus Christ
Through his wonder working power
I know things will be all right

Pastors, bishops, deacons, usher, friends, and members get discouraged when they work hard to get someone back on their feet. That person's marriage, family life, or employment situation was on shaky ground. Once they grabbed hold to a solid foundation then they leave the church congregation or walk out of your life. After all the work you have put into them. They always call when they need something but never show you any support. We sometimes think, "I wish they show me some gratitude. I wish they quit taking up my time when I can be helping my friends or church members."

We have to really pray to God on this because each scenario might be different. God might have placed you in the position, so people learn from you. The people who learn from you can go to carry the gospel to other places. They might fall, but your duties might entail uplifting them. You should do it with a happy servant's smile. Your role might be to get other people ministries started before you are released to build up your ministry. Never get discouraged if their ministry might outgrow yours. Their success is your success. Even if you have only 5 members and they have 2,500 members. Keep believing that the Holy Spirit has not left you, as long as you keep your heart of a servant. God will continue to bless you. Especially, when you do what he wants you to do. After all, we are on the same team.

A servant's smile

Lord, help me with this
Enlighten my understanding on this
I keep spending my time
Helping people get on their feet
My thoughts might be out of line
Then they turn around and leave the church
After all my effort and work
I gave them all I had
Time after time, I welcome them with open arms
They show me no love after they are fed
I know it seems like they don't deserve my time
They only want to call me minister, pastor, etc.
When they need my support
I want to give up
Let them rough it out on their own
Lord plant a righteous decision
For each scenario in my heart
That I might know
When to be their crutch or when to let go
Let me always serve with a smile
Let me enjoy their success
When they fall
Help me lift them up
Also, give me time and strength to encourage your
faithful members of the church
If the unfaithful members call and you want me to go
Let me stay focused on your work
As I go with a servant's smile
To pray for them, their spouse, or child

Some people say, "Give a tenth for tithing." Other people say, "Give as you prosper." Whether we give a tenth or whether we give as we prosper, in either way our giving should be from the heart. Some pastors teach that we can't receive our overflow of blessings without giving an offering or tithing. They have tied the two together like yam with sweet potatoes. We can't tie a spiritual blessing with natural things. It is a great possibility that you could get blessed when you give an offering or tithing, but your spiritual blessings come from lining your thoughts up in prayer with spiritual things.

I'm not suggesting that you quit tithing or giving an offering. If you do it in good moderation with your heart involved, then there is a benefit, but the benefit comes from lining your spiritual thoughts up first. Then, your instincts will allow you to give to God without being forced to do so. An offering to the Lord could be you working for free for his kingdom's benefit. Only God can place in your heart the amount of money that you must contribute to his kingdom.

We should ask the Lord to show us how to give. We shouldn't feel badly if we don't have any money to put in the collection plate because we have taken care of our household. This is one of the main reasons that people miss church because of not having anything to give. In my experiences of not having anything to give, I remember my walks of shame. I was embarrassed walking down the aisle with nothing to give. I felt like everyone was staring at me. My spirit felt low after the highness that I received in Sunday service prior to that point of giving time. This made me feel uncomfortable every time before I realized an offering is much more.

Tithing and Offering

Help me understand tithing and offering
Father what do you consider as tithing?
Father what do you consider as offering?
Everyone has an opinion, but I seek the truth
Bless my heart to know the truth
Let me not lack in this area
If this is something required for us to do
Let my heart give you all that I have
All my love in my heart
Teach me God
Bless me dear God
Let me not withhold anything that is yours
If you require a tenth
Bless me so I can give it
But don't let me be ashamed
If I have nothing to give to you Lord
Let me give you my heart in Jesus' name
If I have been lacking in this area
Father, forgive me, I pray for a change
Let me always give from the heart
Father, give me a better understanding on giving
So I can do my part

One of the hardest things to come to grip with is what associates or close friends to keep in your company when you try to get closer to God. You don't want to abandon everyone. You don't want people to feel like you think you are better than them. You don't want to get sucked in by associates' or close friends' bad influences either. Each case is different because you might be the one to lead others to Christ so isolation for you isn't the answer. You have to ask God to help you with this tricky balance. If you keep the wrong person in your life, then you could backslide into old habits.

Who to keep and who to let go

Lord, who do I keep in my life?
Lord, who do I release from my life?
I'm struggling with this
I don't want to neglect anyone
I don't want it to seem like I'm above anyone
Lord, you hold the plan for my life
I know no one is beneath me
They maybe behind or in front of me
How do I let go friends that I have known all my life?
If they are trying to negatively influence me
Show me the ones I can influence
The ones I can introduce to Christ
I don't want to isolate myself
Not unless you tell me
Right now it is better for my health
Let my heart listen to your voice
That I might not let my associates or friends weigh me
down
That I might have spiritual delight
Whoever I am around
Let me stay connected
So I can draw closer to you
Show me who to keep and who to let go
So I can draw closer to you
That I might stay focused in the right direction
And build up a stronger connection

I know we are supposed to be servants but, in this day, and time, people will take your servanthood for granted. They will try to abuse you and misuse you. There is a fine line to servanthood and being a fool. That is one of the main reason people don't serve one another with the spirit of servanthood. We can't let this block us. The key to life is about being a servant to God and to our neighbors without always wanting gratitude. Even though gratitude from the people we helped causes our heart to be merry. We must remember to keep an attitude of servanthood, even if people don't show us any gratitude. We should eagerly pray for a servant's heart, so we can keep a great attitude.

Difference of being a fool and true servanthood

Guard me against pride
Against acting arrogant
Against acting pessimistic
Against blaming people for no reasons
Against a rebellious heart toward authority
That I might live a life of freedom
In your presence God
Show me how to serve others
Show me how to serve you
Show me how to make a difference for someone else
Show me how to look past self
That I might love you with all my mind, soul, and heart
That I might love my neighbor
As I love you dear God
Protect me from those taking advantage of my
servanthood
That I might do good
Not worrying because you shall enlighten my common
sense
Let your Holy Spirit touch my heart every time I could
Do good, so I won't turn away
From the good I would do
Teach me so I won't get confused
Between the difference of being a fool and true
servanthood

It can get hard sometimes when we discipline our children. They can make us so frustrated at times with their temper tantrums and blowfish syndrome. Some people might say, "What is a blowfish syndrome?" When your child pokes out his or her lips and they blow like a blowfish. If we have a bad temper, then we can easily discipline them the wrong way. Some parents use punishment to keep their children on track. Trying to get our children to follow God by instructing good behavior habits can be tricky. We have to ask our Heavenly Father to guide us, so we can guide our children in the right directions.

My child

Lord, help me teach my child your way
Guide my hands when I discipline my child
Let me keep my composure all the while
Let me know when to chastise my child
Let me know when to discipline my child with a belt
Give me the knowledge, so I can change their bad
behaviors
I don't want my child turning from the right way to the
left
Let me not spare the rod
Guide my hands, so I won't lash out
Out of frustration hitting my child to hard
When there are other alternatives, let me use them
I pray you change my child's heart
Let your peace be in my house, not mayhem
Remove all past inherited curses
Release all your good blessings
Over my child's life and my life
I pray that you keep a protection covering
Over my child day and night

Some people have good advice for everyone else's bad situations. They pray for everyone else's troubles, and it seems to get better. When they look in the mirror, their advice doesn't work for themselves. Their lives are in shambles, and they are surrounded by many troubling situations. They struggle to find answers for their own problems. They attempt everything that they think would work, but they never come to a real solution. Interesting enough, the solution is simple. God have allowed them the gift to help other people, even though it seems quite hard for them to help themselves. They have to go back to the drawing board and ask God to open up their eyes. If their eyes are fully open, then they can see what is holding back their progress and keeping them held prisoner to their situations.

Trying to help self

Lord, I give good advice to everyone else
But I can't even help myself
Am I asking for the wrong thing?
What am I doing wrong?
Am I forgetting to do something?
What is hindering my progress?
Am I being taught a lesson?
Do I need to check myself?
Lord, I ask for help
I seek your advice
Your advice is always right
Help me fix my situations
What is standing in my way?
Do I miss the mark every time I pray?
I seek your counsel
I seek your strength, wisdom, and power
I seek your discretion
Cover my decision
Show me what hinders me
Help me fix it
So my situation won't consume me
I know each scenario isn't the same
Do I need to let go to let you fix it
Make the vision plain
Let me continue to give good advice
I seek your advice
For my troubling situations that occur in my life
Once I receive your advice
Let me consume it and do accordingly to it
In the Mighty name of Jesus Christ

Some people think just because I do good then I will be saved. There is more to it than being just good. It is a great thing if you are a good person. However, have you ever asked yourself, "Why am I a good person? Am I good because I am afraid of the law? Do I do well so people can praise my goodness? Am I a moral man because I don't want people to think I'm unmoral? Do I act well so goodness can come to me?" If you answered yes to either one of those questions, you may have self-goodness. Goodness doesn't save us if we don't act good because we love the Lord. All acts of goodness must be because we love the Lord. The moment we choose to do good to please God not man, and then our goodness counts for something. We can never achieve true goodness on our own because of our impurities. But through Jesus Christ, we can achieve pure goodness.

Why do I act good?

I thought my goodness was something
Until I realize it is nothing
Let my goodness be proving in you
Help me understand goodness
While day and night I pursue you
Let my goodness come naturally
Let me forget about my goodness
Because I'm focused spiritually
As your goodness
Shows up through me
That I maybe good
Not because I am good
But because I can only obtain
Goodness through you
And never by myself alone
Through you Jesus Christ
I can hold on
With goodness by living a righteous life

We get in the habit of setting limitations on our lives. These limitations are set by fear. We say things that hinder our growth in life and in the Lord. They are very common saying that limits us. We must realize that we are speaking things as they are. We have to break away at all costs from those phrases that hold us bound. I listed a few of the phrases that limit us and our prayers. They limit our prayers because we speak limitations over our life before our prayers can be answered.

Limitation Phrases

I'm always broke.   *I can't catch a break.*

I'm always depressed.   *Nobody loves me.*

I can't find a good man or woman.

Example: I asked the Lord to bless my finances. The next day someone asked, "Man let me borrow a dollar." My response was, "I'm always broke."

The negative response isn't showing that I have an enormous amount of faith. I might have set limitations on myself when all I have to do is manage my money wiser. Yet in fact, I believe that I am always broke, but I never asked God the reason why. The majority of times, it is because we are doing something wrong, or we are afraid to step out of our comfort zone.

Limitation Phrases

Lord, I can do all things through you
Let me speak positivity in my life
Let me not deter my prayers
By speaking limitation phrases in my life
Let me respond with faith
Remove fear out of my way
So my prayers can be answered
Increase my love, joy, and faith
Help me believe things as they are
Even though they might seem far
If it is true
And if it is of you
Touch my lips and tongue
Let me answer positively
Knowing blessings will come
Let me speak life in my life
Through your precious name
My Lord Jesus Christ
I destroy anything that holds me bound
I renew myself in you
In you God, I'm profound
I destroy limitations and fear
In you God, I speak things as if they were
It will come to pass as long as you are near

Have you ever been around a person who always has negative things to say? They think someone is always out to do them wrong.

They might say,
"They are always trying to set me up.
That person hates me for no reason.
He or she doesn't like me, and I don't know why.
They must be jealous of me.
The enemy always tries to bring me down."

These comments or phrases can be difficult for us as hearers to consume. You sometimes feel like something is wrong with that person. Have you ever thought about it? There is a possibility of some truth behind the accusations. We'll never know if we don't ask our Father for clarity to see the truth. The truth behind what is going on with that person. Our Father will enlighten us then we can pray for them accordingly. We can pray for that person's healing if they are falsely accusing and blaming other people for their failure. Or we can pray for their situations to improve because they were right all the time.

They might say

Good Father, Father of love
I come on behalf of my friend
You know the one
That thinks negative all the time with no end
Every day there is a story
Someone did this, someone did that
There are no happy moments with any glory
In this person's life
I ask for understanding
Because this person's perceptions maybe wrong or right
I don't know
I'm asking for their healing
I ask that this person grow
I ask that this person outgrow
Their false accusation
But if it is some truth to the matter
I pray you touch their heart and situation
Open my mind to be a better friend
Let me show this person genuine affection
I pray that this person overcome their troublesome
reality
Whatever this maybe
Let them speak with accuracy
Let me comfort them with a humble spirit
Let us both see
The truth as it is and not how we perceive it to be

Sometimes it seems like everyone is against us. We look at people and assume that they are talking about us. These thoughts can put a damper on our day, and it may depress some people. This mindset puts us on guard against the world. Why? Most people say, "They know that people are talking about them because their gut feeling tells them so." We have to be very careful when we base our assumptions off of our emotions. Emotions can be tricky at times, especially when you are not tuned into the correct source.

We have to always do a self-check to make sure our accusations are right before we broadcast it to other people. It may or may not be the case. If we ask God each time in prayer, then he will give us the right conclusion to the matter. Think first and pray before you start blaming people for your life's disappointments. If you are always being unfairly treated, then there could be only two answers. You are the one standing in the need of fixing, or our Heavenly Father is preparing you for something greater. If it is the first one, pray for your self-healing. If it is the second one, pray for peace and joy and thank God for the preparation.

Let me not make false accusations

Open my eyes to see the truth
I think they are plotting against me
I think he or she is envious of me
Is this a trick of my mind?
Why do I think everyone is my enemy?
Or is it true
I don't want to make false accusations
Shine some light that will disprove or prove my theory
I ask you Father
For you know it all
If there is some truth
You will catch me when I fall
If I'm complaining to just be complaining
For no reason at all
Lord, take away this mindset
I want a peace of mind
I want to have a righteous mindset
Lord if the problem isn't them
Then it must be me
Touch my tongue and mind
Renew me
Renew my way of thinking
When these feelings try to set in
In Jesus Name I pray
That all false accusations from my lips end

I know there are women hurting. You have been told false promises too, abused, and misused. You feel as the world is on your shoulders. You are so down in the dump that you accept another woman's trash. You have lost yourself searching for love. On top of that, your children are giving you the blues. You are catching it on both sides because you have to provide for the family. Your divorce or misleading moments don't make you a failure. Sometimes we have to pay the price for our mistakes, but we don't have to stay in that state of mind. The key to happiness isn't finding that perfect mate. You can't build up your self-esteem by whom you are involved with. Past mistakes are past mistakes for a reason. You have to lift your head up high right now. You don't have to go through it alone anymore because God can pull you up and out of your bad situation, negative mindset, and a no-good relationship.

A woman's prayer - Lord, pull me through

Lord, pull me up and out of my situation
Hold my hand
Give me the strength to be a better woman
Touch my heart
I need you in my life
Pull me out of the dark
I don't want a bad relationship anymore
I don't want a negative mindset anymore
I don't want this bad situation
I don't want some other woman's trash
I want all things new
I want to be pleasing to you
Let me deal no more in mess
Help me to rebuild my life
So I can be blessed
Let your peace surround me
Let your joy fulfill me
Help me to patiently wait on you
That you may transform me and my whole life
I will forever be depending on you
Give me peace in my mind
That I might have the faith and hope
That everything in my life will work out in perfect time

When you look in a person eyes, what do you see? Do you see the spirit of that man or are you blinded by his color? Prejudice and racism are hard to escape from to some people for this type of thinking can damage your soul. We have to judge people according to their decisions or judgment call. A Christian is more than being black, white, small, or tall. We are Christians because we make decisions on what God wants us to do. Our Father can help us get rid of prejudice and racism. Our Father sees beyond cultures, ethnicities, and societies. We should give a person a fair chance.

Giving everyone a fair chance

Heavenly Father I come in prayer
Let me look upon every person as my equal
Take the spirit of racism and prejudice out of my soul
Set thou righteousness upon my heart
Let me give everyone a fair chance
Let me base my decision on a righteous decision
Even if that person makes wrong or right decisions
I want to see a person
For that person; not their ethnic or background
Let me give every woman or man
A fair chance
Let me do right in your eyes
Not do right according to my eyes
Because my vision might be blurry
Omnipresence Father
Take away all bigotry
Let me have tolerance for all people
Let me treat each person as my equal
Let your word have the final say so
If I disagree with any man
Let it be because they are trying to pervert the truth
Not opposed by their creed
Help me to love everyone like I love you
If I fall short in loving you
I pray that you jump start my love for you

Many people hardly spend time seeking the advice of our Heavenly Father before they give up on something. We tend to give up when things frustrate us. I'm not talking about things that are contrary to God's word. We should want to give up those things. I'm talking about the things God said it is good.

Some of us might have said,

"I give up on life. I wash my hands with that person. I give up on dating period." A man might say "I wash my hands with all women." A woman might say "I wash my hands with all men."

God said, "His creation was good, and life is good." When we give up or wash our hands, without consulting our Heavenly Father, we give the enemy lead way. The enemy takes this opportunity to mislead us. The enemy replaces the things we give up on with something similar, but the counterfeit is worse than our first situations. Our first situations are the ones we want to give up on without God's approval. It is in most of our nature to replace something decent with something worst. So we have to consult with our Father before we give up on what he said is good.

Don't wash your hands

I'm stuck
There are many issues bothering me
On those issues, I want to give up
But Lord, I am giving them to thee
As I hold the mirror
Lord, let me look in
So, I can see clearer
Why do I feel this way?
On different scenarios
Am I being led astray?
I pray
That you touch my heart
Don't let my emotions imprison me
Let me be acceptable to your truth
Let me be open
To you leading me
Give me a dose of reality
Let your word rule in my life
If is anything that I'm doing wrong
Bring it to the light
Oh my Lord
Help me get right
Give me closure on my concerns
Should I give up or wash my hands
My ears are open, so I may understand
I seek your advice
Take away my frustration
So I can see the goodness of life

Life's pressures cause many people wanting instant relief. Drugs, sex, and alcohol have become a scapegoat for many people. This only satisfies us temporarily while we are waiting on the next fix. Once we are enticed by the feeling, next our emotions become addicted, and then we become dependent on our drug of choice. It is hard to quit on our own will that is why we need our Heavenly Father's divine intervention. We have to keep praying even if we fail the first couple of times, or we will have a relapse. We must keep in mind that only God can give us the strength, which we need to overcome life's pressures.

Fighting the urge

Lord the taste is so sweet to my tongue
Once I please the urge that I was craving
I feel calm
My appetite is killing me slowly
I'm only causing my mind and body harm
When I fulfill my urge
Lord, take away my desire for it
Take away the urge
Let me find no more intense desire in it
Let me find a desire for you
Replace my urge for drugs
With the feeling of contentment in you
I know one touch from you
I will be satisfied
Touch my tongue
Touch my mind
Touch my lungs
Let my drug of choice enter in my body no more
Give me the strength to say no
In Jesus Christ name
Let me forever sustain
Detoxify my system
So that no more drugs remain
Let me not think about it or contemplate
If I get upset or worried
Let me pray to you and meditate
Let my peace in you be my fail-safe

Many people are confused about the body of Christ true definition. They tend to put more emphasis on the geographical assemblies or the church names, which separates us. Societies have woven a blanket over their eyes. Denominational membership is more important than the body of Christ. Many people are at odds with each other over doctrines, worship style, and sectarian allegiance. Some of our churches have become social clubs instead of houses of prayer. They let anything divide them like gender, nationality, and socioeconomics. Everyone claims they have the true way or the truth. Do they really know any truth?

Have you ever noticed that everyone has a creed, doctrinal statements, covenant, confessions, or constitution? So many churches are set up like corporations instead of the houses of prayer. I'm not saying it is wrong or right, but we need to go in our secret place and do some soul searching for truth on all matters of church issues.

Truth on the Matter

Jehovah, I seek truth
Is my worship style pleasing to you?
Am I teaching the right doctrines of truth?
Let us hold no sectarian allegiance
Let us be not separated by gender, nationality, or
socioeconomic
Lord, help me understand your original and new
covenant
Is my creed, doctrinal statements, covenant, confessions,
or constitution pleasing to you?
Help me understand the truth
Teach me how the body of Christ works
Any knowledge I got from my own conclusion
Replace those thoughts with the spirit of truth
Guide me in Jesus Christ name
Touch my hearts, tongue, and lips with the right
qualifications
Lord, touch my lips, so I will not speak a lie
Enlighten my understanding on whom and what to have
tolerance for
That I might be able to explain why
How do we all fit into the body of Christ?
Help me to welcome the truth members
I pray for the ones who are being misled slowly losing
their life

People misunderstand God countless of occasions. I have heard people vent about God in many ways.

Why did God let this happen to me?
If God is God, then my mother, father, child, etc., would have not died?
Why does God let bad things happen to good people?
Why is all the poverty and hunger in the world?
Why does God allow us to do wrong?
Why does God allow people to kill one another?
Why did God allow my spouse to cheat?
Why didn't God protect the children from the storm?

After a while, they start to formulate misinformed opinions about why God isn't good. They stop believing or choose not to believe for those reasons.

God's goodness stretches beyond what we may think. No matter what shape you are in right now. God has allowed you another moment to make your situation better and get an accurate understanding of him.

Have you ever thought of understanding God this way? He is the maker of a top-of-the-line sports car. This car has been rated top notch by the critics. Four people purchased this model. One person jumped in the driver seat and never read the manual. Pistol had the need to go fast so he wrecked his car. We are like this at times because we never read God's manual. If we never read with understanding, our life will be a wreck every time. We just go through life wishing and hoping for something. We never ask God, so we receive nothing.

Another person didn't put enough gas in his car, so Marsheddi had to stop for more gas down the road. Bad things happen to good people because sometimes they forget to keep God first in their lives. God allows us to make mistakes because from our mistakes we learn. Once you run out of gas that first time, then you'll know to keep checking your gas gauge from time to time. Make sure to keep checking your prayer gauge from time to time also.

Another person loved his car, even though Mario knew the car was slowly breaking down. When the motor went out, he just patched it up. It took a tornado to destroy his car before Mario could let go. Once Mario let go, then he received an even greater blessing. Mario received the car he always wanted. God allow storms in our life to prepare us for something greater. A lot of times, we hold on to things that we need to let go. If it wasn't for life's storms, we will be still holding on. The death of a loved one might be your storm. You have to trust God, and he will heal your heart and bless you. Maybe your storm was getting laid off of your job but through our storms we get closer to God.

The last person was badly hurt in an accident because a bus pulled out in front of him. His accident sparked the city to change new laws for better safety. Your painful situation may cause a ripple effect that helps a lot of people. You might have missed a meal so that one day you could inspire other people going through the same situation. By you trusting in God, he is preparing you with ways to break the ice and deliver the truth into people lives.

Does this mean that those sports cars had a default? No by any means, it was accordingly to how those operators operated the cars in their possession that sparked each different result. By the same token, God is still good, but it is how we choose to live our life that sparks different results.

If we could sit down with the maker of those cars, then the maker would give us the dos and don'ts. Just by knowing this, our perspective will greatly be influenced to see that the cars were made well. Very few people get the chance to talk to the carmaker. We are so blessed beyond imagination. We can ask God questions, and he will provide us with answers if we are sincere.

Asking

Lord, why did this happen to me?
Lord, why did my mother, father, child, etc. have to die?
Lord, why does bad things happen to good people?
Lord, why is all the poverty and hunger in the world?
Lord, why do you allow us to do wrong?
Lord, why do you allow people to kill one another?
Lord, why did you allow my spouse to cheat?
Lord, why didn't you protect the children from the storm?
Lord, prepare my heart for the answer
Renew my mind
So I can receive your truth
Take away all my thoughts on these matters
Give me a literal understanding
Please don't let me come to my conclusion

Let me see your straightforward truth
Release me from the bondage of my mind
Correct my perceptions
Help me, so I can understand your goodness
So I can know for myself how good you are
Help me trust in information about you that is reliable
Lord, I'm a little bit confused
Lord, lead my heart to you
Place in my spirit a better understanding of you
That I will know without a doubt
That your love and goodness are true

We sometimes lose the mark. Our vision become blurry with what this world has to offer. Cars, houses, clothing, and money attract our eyesight. Sometimes we try to attain those things with heartaches and disappointments. Through life many trials and troubles, it is so easy to keep our eyes on our bad situations. We must keep ourselves uplifted because we are God's children. We must know that God will take care of us no matter what.

God restores blessings upon his children no matter if we are worthy or unworthy. God's worthy children know that they are loved, so they keep his commandments out of love not fear. God's other children refuse to keep his commandments. They look to themselves for life's answers, which is destruction. We must continue to look to God no matter what our situation looks like.

Look to God is something to remember in your day-to-day struggles or triumphant.

Look to God

Have you been struggling with the day-to-day fights?
Today ask for clarity on your life
What is your purpose and are you fulfilling it according
to his will?
Are you worrying about where you supposed to be right
now?
Stay focused on the goal he has set for you right now
If you trust and obey
You shall get to where you want to go
Let all troubles and cares go
You are sons and daughters of the King
Even if you are not happy with your current situation
Ask, seek, obey, and keep your eyes on the prize with
patience
If you are looked upon as the lowest of the low
Lift your head up high this very moment
Claim your inner glow
Jesus is alive
And we have a right
To live the abundant life
Not to say trouble won't come
Through prayer you will overcome
Tribulation builds character and faith
Keep on trusting
Know he is guiding your way
Sometimes we can't see the city through the fog
But the city still exists, and our God is alive this very day

Prayers for Daily Living

Praying is our food. We must keep a well-balanced diet in order to stay healthy. Our health comes from the word of God and praying to him. I've provided some full course meals that will provide the body with spiritual nourishments on your day-to-day walk. Please meditate and give these nourishments time to digest in your soul.

We don't want to be spiritually malnourished. Let us keep our bodies in great shape by eating our required vitamins of which builds up our energy.

A phrase I like saying is:

I stay connected so I can't be affected

We must stay connected to the power source, so nothing in life will affect us. If life affects us, it will only be for a little while. We know victory is ours by praying for relief in Jesus Christ name. As this relief saturates us, we will surely be full from the spiritual feast and be at total peace.

Lord Touch My Day-to-Day Walk

Lord, touch my day to day walk
Calm the storm
Lord, touch my talk
Let my lips do no harm
Let me live peaceful among all man
In this jungle of life
I look to you morning, noon, and night
Give me the strength to fix my mistakes
Give me strength to forgive
Give me strength to remove all hate
Let peace rule in my life
Let love rule in my life
Give me the strength and willpower to help people
Let people see you through me
Let me be that light shining from the lighthouse
As I walk day to day
Please don't let my light dim out

Bless My Spouse

Father God, bless me with a spouse
Someone who loves you first
Someone who loves me second
Someone who has balance
Balance to serve you God
Balance to enjoy the family life
Holy God, I need a prayer partner
I need someone perfect through you
I want a compassionate spouse
That cares about my feelings
A spouse that loves to have fun
I ask for a spouse that is delightful to the eyes
That is fulfilling to the soul
I want a relationship with my spouse
So, I can talk with my spouse all night
I want to be able to communicate easily with my spouse
I want a spouse on the same page
So we can take vacations and have some money in the
bank
I want a spouse when things go badly
We can pray to you for the answer
I want a spouse when things are going well
We can pray to you for direction
I ask you to heal me
That I might be in the position to receive my spouse
When you bless me with my spouse
Bless our kids
Bless our house

Help Me with My Bills

Lord, I need help with my bills
They are piling up
I don't know which way to turn
I owe the power company again
I owe the insurance man
My bills are increasing
My funds are decreasing
I have maxed out my credit cards
Lord right now times are so hard
My rent is due
I don't know where the money will come from
But God, I'm trusting in you
One thing I do know
If I trust in you
No matter how things look
In the right moment, you will show
You will uplift my spirit
Through you God my finances will grow
My discouragement
Will turn into encouragement
I don't have to beg or plead
My bills will be paid
Because God you supply all my needs

Homeless

Lord, I don't know where I went wrong
I come humble
Asking you to provide me with a home
Not only a shelter for my body
I ask you to touch me
My heart and soul spiritually
I thank you for keeping me thus far
I thank you for protecting me
When I had to sleep in that car
I thank you for the cardboard boxes
That I used as a blanket
I thank you for my warm socks
Lord this day
I pray
For a home
Let me line up with your word
Because today I'm moving on
I have the faith
That you will bless me with a home
Not only a home
But with all life's necessities
In you God
I cling to my sanity
I will no more roam
Because in the very near future
You will provide me with a great home

Peace on the Job

Lord let peace be still on my job
I don't want to have stress
I don't want to work around all this mess
I pray for peace
Let me work in harmony
I pray that you bless my coworkers' life
You know the ones
That always causes strife
I ask that you to bless my boss
Who is always kicking up confusion?
Let peace be still in this place
I pray for real peace not an illusion
Turmoil and depression have to leave here today
I bless the people and bind the devil
I pray for peace and joy on today
I will have a great day
Order my moves through you God
Lead my way
Bless me with peace from day-to-day

Hopelessness

I feel like I can't go on
I feel like my life is worthless
I have no strength to carry on
I'm hopeless
I have no possibility
I have no comfort
I'm surrounded by hostility
My life is filling up with emptiness
God, I know you can wash away those thoughts
My hope can be managed
I'm no longer distraught
I'm finding my solutions in you
I'm finding a brighter future in you
Lord, heal my soul
Renew my mind with hope
I ask for control
Of my negative feelings and emotions
So I can serve you
Bless my mind, body, and soul
That I may be joyful
Praying always, so when any negative feelings arise
I can forever be hopeful

Laid-off

The thoughts of being unemployed is burning in my soul
I trust you God
The unknown is out of my control
Lord, help me deal with these feelings
I know you are guiding my steps
My depressing thoughts are trying to set in
I know by you, I'm kept
I shouldn't be afraid
I wasn't afraid
Until I heard all the people discussing their feelings
I know that I am blessed
I say over and over again
I will let you guide me
Let me block out the enemy's plan
Give me strength
Place peace in my heart
Let me not be afraid of being laid off
In you Lord, I can have a new start
If it is so you will replace my old job
With a much better job
You will keep me
So my family won't starve
By your grace I won't miss a beat
If my company shut their doors
I will land on my feet

Watch Over My Children

Holy Father I come to thee
Humble in prayer
I would like to thank thee
You have blessed me to be a parent
I give my children to thee
Yes, the ones you have given to me
Watch them in the schoolhouse
Watch them in the street
When they get out of line
Correct my children like you corrected me
Show my children your favor
Help me guide them in your ways
Let me shower them with love
I ask for your covering over them for the rest of their
days
Help me teach them how to pray
Let us have a close relationship
But let them have a closer relationship with you
Enlighten their understanding of truth
Let them grow in love and grace
Whether they are happy or sad
Put a smile on their face
Keep their thoughts on you
Fill their heart with love
Let them walk in the ways of truth

Peace in the House

Father God let peace be still
Please let peace be still
In my house, Oh yes, my house
I will forever show you gratitude
I bind this madness
Everyone has an attitude
I bind the rebellion
So our family can climb a higher altitude
I bind frustrations
I bind segregation
So we can communicate like a family
I bind old spoken curses
Any bad thing past down from generation to generation
Lord, fill our home with love
Help us build up a strong foundation
Anything that is not of you
I bind and cast out
Pull my family closer to you
Let us walk after you
Hurt, madness, and frustration
I now subdue
In Jesus Christ Name
I ask for these things
Let peace fill our house
Anything that is the opposite of love
I command it to be thrown out

Help Me Tell the Truth

The words I speak
Is a reflection of me?
My tongue, my tongue
Speak lies that hinder me
I try not to sometimes
But my lips speak them so naturally
I hurt people constantly
Lord, help me control my tongue
Take away the lies and deceit
Renew my heart and mind
Lord, cure me
I don't want to lie ever again
Let me speak truthfully
I am grateful for your salvation
Change my way of thinking
Lies only temporally helped my situation
In you, I can be
I can be the person
You want me to be
I can use my tongue to win souls
Instead of lying out of control

I Need Food

Lord, I don't know
Where my next meal will come from
I'm trusting and believing
I'm waiting on a miracle
I know you will provide
I prayed this morning
When I open my eyes
I have spent all my money on gas
We have eaten our last bread
I will not go hungry
As long as I trust in thee
I pray for food
Enough to feed my family
You have never let me down
As I open or close my eyes from prayer
You can be found
You provide my spiritual food
As well as my natural food
God let me stay in your will
I thank you in advance for my next meal

Seeking Employment

I applied for a job today
My applications are being denied
I'm still seeking employment anyway
Lord, bless my résumé
Touch my cover letter
With you in the mix
I can't help but do better
Touch my lips in the interview
Help me with the correct attire
Let me smile
Cover me so I can be hired
I seek employment
Please be in my mist
I can be president
With you helping me
I have limitless possibilities
I won't be unemployed for long
Show me what to do
So I can move right along
Let me leap into action
Following your instructions
Taking your correction to heart
I seek you Lord
I seek a steady job

Live Right

My life is bruised
It has been misused
I need a touch from my Father
I need a touch from my Savior
I need a touch from you
I feel my desire
I want to get to know you
I want to know you God
I want a change
Change my life
I repent because
I haven't been living right
I want to be a part of your family
I want to love you more
I want to know about your love for me
I want to accept you
I thank you for already accepting me
I thank you for my life
I thank you for your son
Who died, so I can have eternal life
He now lives and I can live through him
I praise you, with all my might

Depressed

I can lift up my head
Take away my stress
Let hurt live no more in my life
I bind the feelings of being depressed
I have a Father
That owns everything
I don't have to want for anything
He will provide
I am more than less
I am much greater
I'm a child of God
He has touched my heart
He gives me peace and joy
I just have to reclaim my feelings and thoughts
Place them back in the master's hand
Lord, take away my feelings of depression
Suicide has no place in my thoughts
I bind suicide and depression
In Jesus Name
Let your peace, joy, and happiness remain
My hurt might last for a day and night
But tomorrow is a new day
I embrace it with love and hope
As I cast my worries away when I pray

Right Motives

Touch the person who is sitting in the church
That has the wrong motives
Touch their motives
Let us show so much love
That they are consumed
Let the enemy have no place in their heart
I pray for their brand-new start
They are spies
Lord, open their eyes
Let the Holy Spirit hit them
That it might awaken them to a new life
Let the truth come into their heart
Whatever evil motives they harbor
It must depart
We release good things
We bind any evil thing
Free that person or persons to life
We ask all these things
In the name of Jesus Christ

My Child's Scholarship

Lord, you know my situation
I want my child to further her education
Bless my child with an ongoing relationship
With you Heavenly Father
Bless my child with a paid for scholarship
Let my child never forget you
Help her grow in your favor
For Lord, I know you are able
Bless my child's study habits
Bless my child's mindset
Let her have a life of balance
With love and admiration for you God and deep respect
Lord, you know I don't have the funds right now
I'm asking that you show up some way or somehow
I ask in Jesus Christ name
Bless my child with a fully paid scholarship
Today I will proclaim
I believe you will do it
In the mighty Jesus Christ name

More Faith

I bind the evil that is in my life
Lord, confuse the devil because he doesn't have a right
A right to attack me with fear
I plead the blood of Jesus
Overall unhappiness and fear
I bind the evilness of my flesh
Let me overcome it
With the presence of the Holy Spirit
Increase my faith
Let faith rule in my life
Keep me focused on your love Heavenly Father that you
have shown us in Jesus Christ
When I receive the notice in the mail
Let not my faith fail
Let me not misplace my faith because of my conditions
Let me pray and obey then receive impossible results
Because your Almighty power has no restrictions

What do I need to do?

Lord, what are you saying to me?
Let me hear clearly
Place within me a teachable spirit
What are your plans for my life?
Open my heart, eyes, and ears, so I can be aware of it
Let your peace come upon me, so I can delight
Take away all distractions
Take away all fear
That has me focusing on the natural
Let me have faith in the impossible
Your healing power is supernatural
Let me be mindful
To always count on your word
When things are joyful or stressful
I pray for the impossible
For I know the possible can be done
The impossible can be done through Jesus Christ
Let me understand your presence in my life
Whatever you call me to do
Let me jump into action
Releasing all possibilities
Entrenched with your blessings

From Life to Life

Lord, I'm grieving right now
Over my loved one that departed
Let your peace fill my heart
Only you can help me through this
On my own, I don't know where to start
Comfort me through this moment
Comfort my family members through this moment
Let us find our joy in you
If it is anything, we don't understand
Show us the way
Lord, hold our hands
Let your presence be felt
We need your friendship
Because we can't do it ourselves
Dry our eyes
Wash our tears
Let us reflect on you
Keep us in your presence
So we can soak up your joy
Ease my mind
I pray for peace
Lord, console and reassure me
Because only in you
I can find relief in my life
Through Jesus Christ
I can smile
Because I understand the meaning
(John 11:25-26)

Locked Down

I hear the bars slam close
Lord, forgive me
I pray for my soul
I am surrounded by inmates
I can't go to sleep
Lord watch over me
Please give me peace
Help me to find you
As I stare at the four walls
Let me stand up for you
Like I stood up in the world for myself
I repent over past sins
Lord, I realize you are the only friend I have left
I pray for protection from the enemy
Guard me with your spiritual army
Give me a peace of mind
Let me stay focused on you
While I do my time
Cleanse my spiritual house
So I won't make the same mistakes
Once I get out
Help me be a productive individual in society
So I can tell the world how you rescued me

Another way to build up on your spiritual calorie count is to say a prayer before you read his word. Then after you read his word, you should meditate on the promises from God. God can't lie and all his words will come to pass. If he spoke it to you, then it shall be.

Pray before reading

Lord, help me to understand
What I read
In the way you want me to understand
Before I proceed
Give me wisdom and spiritual insight
That I may be able to plant a truth seed
In my life
And
In someone else's life

<u>You can make it simple as possible</u>

Like: LORD, HELP ME UNDERSTAND THIS!

Pray after reading

Lord, help me maintain this valuable information
Let your Holy Spirit call it to my memory
If I need it in any situation
Let your truth soak in
Let my self-knowledge be removed out
So that I may understand your word without a doubt

Romans 10:9(NKJV)

⁹ that if you confess with your mouth the Lord Jesus and believe in your heart that God has raised Him from the dead, you will be saved

I Confess

I have confessed you Lord
I believe in my heart that you are my Lord
I believe on the third day that you were raised from the dead
Jesus, I call on your mighty name
Help me understand salvation
Help me understand regeneration
I know I am saved
But my emotions are the same
Help me to understand baptism
Some of my old ways remain
I know my sins were washed in your blood
I felt the spirit
Afterwards the congregation gave me a hug
Now, I am all alone
Jesus, show me
What is right or wrong?
I need a touch from you
Guide me in your light
I want to be your disciple
I seek understanding of the truth
Jesus, I publicly confess my love for you
Reveal to me
All that I must continue do

Philippians 4:19 (NKJV)
[19] And my God shall supply all your need according to His riches in glory by Christ Jesus.

Romans 8:37 (NKJV)
[37] Yet in all these things we are more than conquerors through Him who loved us.

John 14:27(NKJV)
[27] Peace I leave with you, My peace I give to you; not as the world gives do I give to you. Let not your heart be troubled, neither let it be afraid.

Proverbs 1:33 (NKJV)
[33] But whoever listens to me will dwell safely, And will be secure, without fear of evil."

John 15:7-11 (NKJV)
[7] If you abide in Me, and My words abide in you, you will ask what you desire, and it shall be done for you. [8] By this My Father is glorified, that you bear much fruit; so you will be My disciples. [9] "As the Father loved Me, I also have loved you; abide in My love. [10] If you keep My commandments, you will abide in My love, just as I have kept My Father's commandments and abide in His love. [11] "These things I have spoken to you, that My joy may remain in you, and *that* your joy may be full

Your Word Said

Your word says,
"Father, you supply all my needs"
My needs are supplied
Your word says, "We are more than conquerors"
I can conquer anything through you Jesus
Your word says, "Let not my heart be troubled neither
afraid"
I won't be troubled or afraid
Your word says, "Whoever listens to you will dwell
safely, and secure, without fear of evil"
I will dwell safely and secure, without fear of evil
Your word says, "Your joy remains in me and whatever
I ask according to your will, it shall be done if I keep
your commandments"
I stand on your promises
Help me keep your commandments
I pray that I line up my life
In every way that I may receive all of the wonderful
promises
You provide for me
Keep me in the center of your presence
In the natural as well as spiritually
For there is no greater love
Than what you did for me (John 3:16)
I pray today
Contemplating on the thoughts of what your word says

More Love

Let me teach my foes in love
For love is power
In you all my power resides
You are my power source
Through your love, I can recognize
My life is slowly changing
I am changing into a better me
I can feel the warmness from the Holy Spirit
You have sent to guide me
My thoughts are no more the same
I thank you Lord
I praise Lord
I come before your throne
Not because something is wrong
But because everything is going right
Thank you Lord for blessing me
Because everything is alright
I enjoy talking to you
Bless me to be able to continue to talk with you
Bless me to be able to continue to fall deeper in love with
you
Unlock the keys to my heart's chambers with your love
Enrich your presence in my life with your love
Let us share a magnificent experience each day
Let me give you praise just for waking me up to see
another day

Conclusion

Prayer does work and will continue to work. The million-dollar question is does your faith work? If we lack faith, then our prayers won't work. Do we obey our Father? Do we have a heart filled with love or hatred? Do we set up enough time to communicate with him? Your soul rest in his hands, therefore we must outstretch our hand to get to know him. There is truly power in prayer because we overcome self through him. He can become a closer friend if we let him. A friend that never shares or listens is not a friend.

We have a Savior who listens and will give us good advice if we only take time to talk to him. I invite you to open up your heart, your world, and your life to him. Please give Jesus Christ a chance to enhance your life by praying to the Father in his name. The impossible will be possible because countless blessings rain on the earnest man or woman of prayer. Pray to understand, pray to give thanks, pray for truth, pray for help, pray for others, or pray for self but continue to pray with no delay. *May our Almighty Omnipresence Father* bless you with a word to say and a thought to pray!

Also available from Lorenzo C Spencer

7 Prayers for Your Spiritual Life

A Young Black Man

Blessings for Generations
Mother Teach Me How to Pray

Blessings for Generations
A Christmas Love Story

I hope this book was a blessing to you

Never Stop Praying

May God Always Keep You
In his peace
In his Joy
And
In his love

www.ingramcontent.com/pod-product-compliance
Lightning Source LLC
La Vergne TN
LVHW051039080426
835508LV00019B/1597